The

God's Call

To

Leave

Secret Societies

by Tommy Arbuckle

Foreword

"*The Answer: God's Call To Leave Secret Societies*" is a God-breathed literary work of art. This book, authored by a trusted and experienced Minister, is sifted through godly wisdom and birthed through human experience as it delves into the spiritual deception that surrounds secret societies. Most importantly, it painstakingly highlights what makes such spiritually dangerous organizations so alluring. This is mainly for those who are unaware of the deep, dark, dangerous, and destructive end that awaits those who negligently fail, or rebelliously refuse, to confess, renounce, repent, and leave! This book is a priceless jewel that provides a biblical basis for anyone who belongs to a secret society to accurately assess their perilous position and be able to make the right decision. The right decision is to repent by turning away from such soul-destroying organizations. Moreover, this godly work is a practical tool that demonstrates how crying out to God for guidance leads to healing and ultimate deliverance from the powers of darkness.

"*From the solemn ceremonies of Freemasonry to the lively traditions of college fraternities and sororities,*" this book fearlessly and unabashedly exposes the proverbial "*tricks of the trade*" that make it easy for innocent and well-intentioned people to be deceived into calling God's wrath upon themselves by joining organizations that require allegiance through oaths and secrecy. The **Holy Spirit** of **Christ Jesus** uses **Minister Tommy** to reveal one of the surest ways to anger **God** and unwittingly invite His wrath and just judgment by swearing allegiance to and/or serving

3

other gods in direct contraventions of **Exodus 20:3-5**. He delves into the religious deception and spiritual blindness that comes from taking secret oaths and bowing down before evil altars that effectuate the unwitting selling of innocent souls to *Satan*.

This extraordinary book identifies the soul-destroying dangers of belonging to secret societies and shares words of wisdom (**I Corinthians 12:8**) and battle-tested practical steps to be completely delivered from the enemy's snare. One such scripture-based practical step, which is my personal favorite, centers around **Isaiah 5:20**, which reads **"Woe to those who call evil good, and good evil; Who put darkness for light, and light for darkness; Who put bitter for sweet, and sweet for bitter!"** (**NKJV**) The **Holy Spirit** richly blessed *Brother Tommy* to convert this very passage of scripture into a powerful soul-saving prayer that's based upon **James 1:5**, which reads **"If any of you lacks wisdom, let him ask of God, who gives to all liberally and without reproach, and it will be given . . ."** (**NKJV**) This scripture is the very essence of this book. Namely, God's wisdom, knowledge, understanding, grace, mercy, justice, blessings for obedience, (**Deuteronomy 11:29**) curses for disobedience, (Id.), healing, deliverance, and most importantly, soul salvation, are open and available to everyone, not only a select few. Please buckle up for the ride of your (eternal) life!

Pastor A.W. Barlow, Esquire, Breakthrough Prayer Ministries, Jacksonville, Florida

Author's Autograph

About The Author

*Minister **Tommy Arbuckle*** is a prophetic teacher, author, intercessor, entrepreneur, and mentor called by God to be a leader in both business and ministry. He's uniquely gifted in street and marketplace evangelism. His ministry is marked by healing, miracles, signs, and wonders that draw others into faith in ***Jesus Christ***.

During his college years, he joined *Prince Hall Freemasonry* in 1994 and *Omega Psi Phi Fraternity, Inc.* in 1995. However, in the Fall of 2022, **God** revealed he had to renounce and denounce his membership in all secret societies to be pleasing to Him. This pivotal revelation and decision deepened his commitment to walking in God's truth and helping others do the same. Passionate about seeing every member within the body of **Christ** walking in the fullness of their measure, *Minister Tommy* is dedicated to empowering believers to be about the *Father's* business. His teachings and mentorship inspire **Christians** to embrace their God-given potential and live out their faith boldly in every sphere of life.

He's married and has six (6) daughters and (6) grandchildren. He resides in *Peoria, Illinois*, and loves hunting and fishing in his free time.

Table of Contents

Introduction

Chapter 1

The Allure of Secrecy pg. 13

Chapter 2

Unveiling Freemasonry, Fraternities & Societies pg. 17

Chapter 3

The Genesis of Prince Hall Freemasonry & Black Greek Letter Organizations pg. 29

Chapter 4

The Biblical Perspective on Secret Societies pg. 35

Chapter 5

The History of Idolatry & False Religions pg. 39

Chapter 6

Satan, the Architect of Secret Societies pg. 51

Chapter 7

Unveiling the Idolatrous and False Religious Nature of Secret Societies pg. 63

Chapter 8

Altars, Rituals, Oaths and Covenants pg. 69

Table of Contents continued...

Chapter 9

Consequences of Participation pg. 87

Chapter 10

From Bonds to Liberation: A Testimony of Renouncing Secret Societies pg. 93

Chapter 11

Embracing God's Call to Holiness pg. 132

Additional Resources pg. 137

Introduction

The Answer: God's Call To Leave Secret Societies

"And have no fellowship with the unfruitful works of darkness, but rather reprove them. For it is a shame even to speak of those things which are done of them in secret." (Ephesians 5:11-12 KJV)

Secret societies have held a captivating allure throughout history, beckoning individuals with promises of belonging, influence, and hidden knowledge. With its ancient traditions and elaborate rituals, *Freemasonry* often stands at the forefront of discussions surrounding secret societies. While some view it as a harmless fraternal organization, others raise concerns about its rituals, symbolism, and oaths, which may inadvertently challenge *Christian* convictions. Similarly, fraternities and sororities, prevalent in collegiate settings, offer a sense of community and belonging. However, the rituals and practices associated with these groups may inadvertently stray from *Christian* values, prompting questions about the compatibility of allegiance to **God** and them. For some, mentioning secret societies like *Freemasonry*, fraternities, and sororities may evoke curiosity or confusion. These clandestine organizations have long held a place in society's shadows, shrouded in mystery and allure. Yet, beneath the surface lies a truth that beckons to be unearthed. Whether you're unfamiliar with secret societies or deeply entrenched within their ranks, this book invites you to explore the complexities of allegiance, belonging, and spiritual integrity associated with them.

As I reflect on my journey through life, I'm compelled to share with you a narrative that intertwines personal experience with profound revelation. It's a story of seeking belonging, navigating cultural & societal pressures, and ultimately discovering the true path to be pleasing in the eyes of God apart from secret societies. For many years, my family and I were involved in secret societies on some level or another. As a member of *Freemasonry* and a fraternity, I was captivated by the promises of camaraderie, influence, and opportunity for success. I was lured in by my family's history of involvement, and the mystique added to the sense of belonging that these organizations seemed to offer. I longed to be numbered among other great *African American* professionals who were members whom I looked up to. The constant bombardment as a child of having to be told you could be something by my parents and teachers who suffered racial mistreatment during the sixties made me want to achieve greatness. But my story isn't unique. For many individuals like me, particularly within marginalized communities of the *African American* community in America, the allure of secret societies often stems from a deep-seated need for belonging and acceptance. In a society rife with racial mistreatment and discrimination, the desire to find a sense of camaraderie and success can lead individuals down paths they may later regret.

As I delved deeper into these realms of secrecy, rituals, and oaths, I grappled with a profound realization: my allegiance to these societies may have inadvertently distanced me from my faith and true purpose in **God**. Despite the camaraderie and networking opportunities,

I couldn't shake the feeling of spiritual unease that lingered within me when I considered them. My journey took a pivotal turn in April of 2022 when I embarked on a quest for truth, guided by the light of *Christian* morality and biblical principles. Through introspection, discernment, and revelation, I came to understand the inherent conflicts between my involvement in secret societies and my devotion to God.

For those of you who may be unfamiliar with secret societies like *Freemasonry*, fraternities, and sororities, allow me to illuminate the rituals, symbolism, and oaths that characterize these societies. While they may appear innocuous on the surface and say they're founded on "*Christian* principles," a closer examination of them reveals conflicts with this statement. To my brothers and sisters currently involved in these organizations, I extend a heartfelt plea: consider the implications of the oaths you've taken and the allegiances you've sworn. Are they in alignment with your faith and your relationship with **God**? Are they worth compromising your spiritual integrity and moral convictions? Is **God** pleased with the organization and your involvement as a member? It's never too late to reassess your path and realign your life with God's will. Through introspection, prayer, and the guidance of the **Holy Spirit**, you can find the courage to renounce the ungodly oaths you've taken and denounce these organizations publicly.

As we embark on this journey together, I urge you to deeply reflect on your own experiences and motivations. This introspection will help you understand how cultural and societal pressures and the longing for belonging may have influenced your decisions. It's crucial to recognize that true fulfillment can only be found in aligning our lives with the will of **God**. This alignment isn't a daunting task but a path that leads to true fulfillment and spiritual growth. The revelations shared within these pages aim to inspire, courage, give clarity, convict, and a renewed commitment to holiness in the eyes of **God**. As we delve into the depth of this contentious issue, humble yourself and prepare your heart to seek understanding, discernment, and ultimately clarity from **God**. Let us embark on this quest for truth together, embracing the transformative power of **God's** love and guidance in our lives.

1

"God is going to judge everything we do, whether good or bad, even things done in secret" (Ecclesiastes 12:14 GNT)

Secret societies have a magnetic appeal, drawing individuals into their fold with promises of belonging, influence, and hidden knowledge. From the shadows of history to the bustling corners of contemporary society, these enigmatic organizations have captured the imagination of many.

At their core, secret societies offer a sense of exclusivity—a feeling of being part of something special, something beyond the ordinary. For those who have felt marginalized or disconnected, the allure of belonging to such a group can be irresistible. It's a chance to find camaraderie to forge bonds with like-minded individuals who share similar aspirations and values. Moreover, secret societies often promise opportunities for advancement and success. Whether through networking connections, access to resources, or the acquisition of esoteric knowledge, members believe their affiliation will open doors to new possibilities. In a world where competition is fierce and opportunities are scarce, the allure of such benefits cannot be underestimated. Yet, it's the element of secrecy that perhaps holds the most significant appeal. The veiled rituals, cryptic symbols, and whispered oaths create an aura of mystery and intrigue, drawing individuals deeper into the fold. The thrill of uncovering hidden truths and participating in clandestine activities can be intoxicating, fueling a sense of excitement and belonging unlike any other. But beneath the surface of this allure lies a darker reality—one that's often overlooked or ignored. The secrecy that binds members together can also serve to conceal questionable practices or ideologies. What begins as innocent curiosity or a desire for community can quickly spiral into something more sinister, as individuals find themselves ensnared in webs of deceit and manipulation. Moreover, the very nature of secrecy can foster an environment of mistrust and division. As members are sworn to maintain confidentiality and allegiance to the group above all else, relationships outside of society may suffer. Family, friends, and even one's conscience can become casualties of this allegiance, as individuals prioritize the interests of society over all else. It's crucial for you, as a reader, to be cautious and aware of these potential pitfalls in your spiritual journey, as they can lead to compromising your integrity, morality, and spiritual well-being.

In exploring the allure of secrecy, it's essential to recognize the potential dangers and pitfalls that lie ahead. While the promises of belonging, success, and hidden knowledge may be enticing, they come with a cost—one that's often paid in compromises to one's integrity, morality, and spiritual well-being. In the pages that follow, we'll delve deeper into the complexities of secret societies, examining their origins, rituals, and impact on individuals and society at large. Through careful analysis and reflection, we'll uncover the truth behind the allure of secrecy and the consequences of succumbing to its seductive charms. This process of reflection and analysis is crucial in understanding the allure of secrecy and its potential dangers, as it allows us to see beyond the surface and comprehend the deeper implications of our choices.

2

"Thou hast set our iniquities before thee, our secret sins
in the light of thy countenance" (Psalm 90:8 KJV)

Freemasonry

From the dawn of civilization, secret societies have
held a captivating allure, drawing individuals into their
enigmatic fold with promises of belonging, influence,
and hidden knowledge. These organizations, with their
ancient roots deeply embedded in our history, have
thrived on the allure of secrecy and exclusivity. At their
core, secret societies are defined by their clandestine
nature, operating behind closed doors and shrouded in
mystery. The very concept of secrecy creates an aura
of intrigue, enticing individuals to seek membership in
pursuit of something beyond the ordinary.

One of the most well-known and influential secret
societies is *Freemasonry*. Tracing its origins back to
medieval stonemason guilds, *Freemasonry* has
evolved into a global fraternal organization with
millions of members worldwide. Central to
Freemasonry is the belief in brotherhood, morality, and
the pursuit of self-improvement. They're characterized
by their elaborate rituals, symbols, and degrees.
Initiation ceremonies mark the beginning of a
member's journey, with each degree representing a
stage of spiritual and moral enlightenment. Through
rituals such as the *"Entered Apprentice"* and *"Master
Mason"* degrees, members are imparted with moral
lessons and philosophical teachings. Despite its

philanthropic endeavors and emphasis on moral virtue, *Freemasonry* has faced its share of controversies. Critics allege that its secretive nature breeds elitism and exclusivity, while conspiracy theories abound regarding its purported influence in politics and finance.

Fraternities & Sororities

In the realm of collegiate life, fraternities and sororities hold a prominent place within this type of society. Touted as social organizations, these entities typically found on college campuses, provide students with a sense of community, camaraderie, and networking opportunities. Fraternities and sororities are known for their rituals, traditions, and symbols, which serve to foster a sense of identity and belonging among members. Initiation ceremonies, known as "**pledging**," mark the beginning of a member's journey and often involve various rites of passage.

While fraternities and sororities promote ideals of leadership, service, and scholarship, they have also faced scrutiny for their culture of hazing, alcohol abuse, and exclusivity. In recent years, incidents of misconduct and discrimination have prompted calls for reform within these organizations.

Rituals & Practices

Central to the identity of secret societies are their rituals and practices, which serve to reinforce values, foster camaraderie, and impart esoteric knowledge. From the solemn ceremonies of *Freemasonry* to the lively traditions of college fraternities and sororities, rituals play a crucial role in shaping the identity and culture of these organizations. Rituals often involve what is believed to be symbolism, and allegory, drawing on ancient traditions and mystical teachings. Through participation in rituals, members are initiated into the secrets and mysteries of the society, forging bonds of brotherhood and sisterhood that transcend the mundane world.

Impact On Members

Membership in secret societies can have a profound impact on individuals, shaping their beliefs, values, and relationships. For many, membership offers a sense of belonging and identity, providing a supportive community in times of need. However, the influence of secret societies in an individual's life can have drawbacks. The required time commitments and associated dues can conflict with other priorities. The culture of secrecy can breed mistrust and divisiveness, alienating members from their families, friends, and communities. The pressures of conformity and loyalty can lead individuals to compromise their integrity and moral convictions.

Controversies & Criticisms

Throughout history, secret societies have been subject to scrutiny and criticism, often accused of fostering elitism, corruption, and secrecy. From allegations of conspiracies to concerns of abuse of power, these organizations have faced their share of controversies.

In recent years, calls for transparency and accountability have grown louder, prompting secret societies to reassess their practices and adapt to changing societal norms. While some have embraced reform and greater openness, others continue to operate behind closed doors, shielding their activities from public scrutiny. In the face of criticism and controversy, the allure of secret societies remains as potent as ever. Yet, as we peel back the layers of secrecy and examine their impact on individuals and society, it becomes clear that the truth behind these organizations may not be as glamorous as it seems.

Exploring Freemasonry's Contradictions With Christianity

Freemasonry, often regarded as a venerable institution rooted in tradition and fraternity, presents a complex tapestry of beliefs, rituals, and symbolism. However, when examined through the lens of **Christianity**, inherent contradictions and tensions emerge, challenging the compatibility between *Freemasonry* and the **Christian** faith.

1. Theistic Pluralism versus Christian Exclusivity

At the heart of *Freemasonry* is a belief in the "*Grand Architect of the Universe*" or the "*Supreme Being*," which serves as a unifying principle among its diverse members. While *Freemasonry* doesn't endorse a specific religion, it requires its members to affirm a belief in a higher power. This concept of the *Supreme Being* is intentionally vague and inclusive, allowing individuals from various religious backgrounds to participate. However, from a **Christian** perspective, this concept of the *Supreme Being* contradicts the exclusive nature of the **Christian God** as revealed in the **Bible**. Christianity teaches that salvation is found only through **Jesus Christ**, and the worship of any other deity is considered idolatry. Thus, *Freemasonry's* affirmation of a generic higher power undermines the fundamental **Christian** belief in the uniqueness and sovereignty of **God**.

One of the notable figures in *Freemasonry* was *Albert Pike*. In his book "*Morals and Dogma of the Ancient and Accepted Scottish Rite of Freemasonry*," Pike makes several statements that indicate his view of *Freemasonry* as a religious institution. One of the most frequently cited quotes is: "***Every Masonic Lodge is a temple of religion, and its teachings are instruction in religion***." This quote is found in "***Morals and Dogma***," which Pike published in 1871. *Albert Pike* was a prominent *Masonic* scholar, and his writings have significantly influenced the beliefs and practices within *Freemasonry*, especially in the Scottish Rite.

Freemasonry also espouses a philosophical viewpoint centered around the concepts of the "***Fatherhood of God and the Brotherhood of Man***." This principle suggests that all men are brothers under the fatherhood of a single, universal deity. *Freemasonry* teaches that this singular God is worshiped by individuals from diverse religious backgrounds, each referring to the divine by different names and through various rituals. This inclusive stance is designed to foster unity and camaraderie among men of all religious beliefs, emphasizing moral and ethical development over specific doctrinal adherence. However, this view of a universal deity accessed through multiple religious paths directly contradicts core **Christian** teachings, which assert the exclusivity of **God** as revealed through **Jesus Christ**. Christianity holds that salvation and true knowledge of God are available only through **Jesus Christ**, directly challenging the *Masonic* doctrine of a universally accessible God recognized under many names and forms.

2. Secretive Oaths & Rituals

Freemasonry is characterized by its elaborate rituals, ceremonies, and oaths, which are shrouded in secrecy and symbolism. Initiation into *Freemasonry* involves taking solemn vows and participating in rituals that are meant to impart moral and philosophical lessons. Many of these rituals and oaths involve **"swearing"** allegiance to *Freemasonry* above all else, often with dire consequences for those who betray their vows. From a **Christian** perspective, such oaths can conflict with the biblical commandment to **"swear not at all"** (**Matthew 5:34**) and the admonition against making vows that cannot be fulfilled (**Matthew 5:37**). The secretive nature of *Freemasonry* raises questions about transparency and accountability, particularly considering the biblical principle of living in the light and avoiding works of darkness (**Ephesians 5:11-13**).

One of the well-known oaths taken in *Freemasonry* is the *Entered Apprentice* oath. Here is an example of the oath taken by new members when they first join the fraternity: "***I, [name], of my own free will and accord, in*** *the presence of Almighty God, and this Worshipful Lodge, erected to Him and dedicated to the Holy Saints John, do hereby and hereon solemnly and sincerely promise and swear, that I will always hail, ever conceal, and never reveal any of the secrets, arts, parts, or points of the hidden mysteries of Ancient Freemasonry, which have been heretofore, shall be at this time, or may at any future period be communicated to me as such, to any person or persons whomsoever, except it be to a true and lawful Brother Mason, or within the body of a just and legally constituted Lodge of Masons; and neither unto him nor them until by strict trial, due examination, or lawful Masonic information, I shall have found him or them as lawfully entitled to the same as I am myself. All this I most solemnly and sincerely promise and swear, with a firm and steadfast resolution to perform the same, without any equivocation, mental reservation, or secret evasion of mind whatsoever, binding myself under no less penalty than that of having my throat cut across, my tongue torn out by its roots, and buried in the rough sands of the sea, at low water mark, where the tide ebbs and flows twice in twenty-four hours, should I ever knowingly or willingly violate this my solemn Obligation of an Entered Apprentice Mason. So help me God and keep me steadfast in the due performance of the same.*"

This oath is one of the several that *Freemasons* take at various stages of their progression through the degrees of *Freemasonry*. Each degree has its own set of oaths and obligations, often with symbolic penalties attached to emphasize the seriousness of the commitments made.

3. Esoteric Teachings & Symbolism

Freemasonry is steeped in esoteric symbolism and teachings, drawing on ancient mystical traditions and philosophical principles. Symbols such as the square and compass, the apron, and the all-seeing eye hold deep significance within *Masonic* rituals and ceremonies. While *Freemasonry* claims to promote moral virtue and enlightenment, some of its teachings and symbolism can conflict with **Christian** doctrine. For example, the concept of "***The Great Architect of the Universe***" may be interpreted as a form of deism or pantheism, which stands in contrast to the biblical understanding of God as a personal and transcendent being. The emphasis on self-improvement and enlightenment within *Freemasonry* can potentially lead individuals away from reliance on God's grace and the transformative power of the ***Holy Spirit***, which are central tenets of the **Christian** faith.

Freemasonry's use of biblical figures in its teachings creates an illusion of alignment with the **Bible**. Individuals like Tubal-Cain, a descendant of Cain mentioned in the **Bible** in ***Genesis 4:22***, is recognized as an instructor of every craftsman in bronze and iron. Tubal-Cain is symbolically significant in *Freemasonry*, representing skill, craftsmanship, and the industrious spirit. Due to his attributes, Tubal-Cain is presented as a master craftsman, linking *Freemasonry* to the ancient tradition of craftsmanship. In addition, *King Solomon*, revered for building the Temple, is often referenced to give *Freemasonry* a semblance of biblical legitimacy. *King Solomon* being David's son was instructed by his father to build the Temple. Despite his initial devotion to **God** and the construction of the Temple, *King Solomon* eventually fell into idolatry by following the false gods of his many foreign wives. This disobedience occurred after **God** appeared to him twice, warning him to remain faithful (***1 Kings 11:9-10***). Consequently, **God** was displeased with Solomon and declared the kingdom would be torn away from him (***1 Kings 11:11***). King Solomon's years serve as a poignant reminder of the dangers of turning away from God and the severe consequences that follow such actions.

Using figures like Tubal-Cain and *King Solomon* within Freemasonry creates an appearance of alignment with **Christian** values, thereby deceiving people into thinking it's a **Christian** organization. However, it's misleading because *Freemasonry* fundamentally believes that all religions stem from the same God and promotes a universalistic view of spirituality. This inclusive philosophy contrasts sharply with Christianity's exclusive claims about **Jesus Christ** as the only way to **God** (***John 14:6***). By incorporating biblical references, *Freemasonry* creates a veneer of *Christian* legitimacy while simultaneously promoting beliefs that are inconsistent with biblical Christianity.

4. Exclusivity & Discrimination

Freemasonry has historically been criticized for its exclusivity and discrimination despite its stated principles of brotherhood and equality. Women and atheists are typically excluded from membership, and certain religious beliefs may be incompatible with *Freemasonry's* requirements. From a **Christian** perspective, such exclusivity and discrimination raise concerns about the impartiality of *Freemasonry* and its adherence to the biblical principle of showing no favoritism or partiality (***James 2:1-9***).

In response to the exclusionary practices of mainstream *Freemasonry* and collegiate fraternities and sororities, marginalized communities within the *African American* community in America sought to create avenues for fellowship, advancement, and empowerment. *Prince Hall Freemasonry*, named after its founder *Prince Hall*, was established in the late 18th century as a separate branch of *Freemasonry* to provide *African Americans* with the opportunity to participate in the fraternal order. Similarly, *Black Greek Letter Fraternities & Sororities*, commonly known as the *Divine Nine*, emerged in the early 20th century to offer *African American* college students a sense of belonging and community amidst the racial discrimination prevalent on campus. These organizations were founded on principles of brotherhood, sisterhood, and service, providing a platform for *African Americans* to thrive and succeed in a society where opportunities for advancement were often limited by systemic racism and prejudice. We'll go into greater depth about these historical black organizations in the next chapter.

In conclusion, while *Freemasonry*, fraternities, and sororities may offer fellowship, moral teachings, and a sense of belonging to its members, its core beliefs, rituals, and practices present significant contradictions with the **Christian** faith. For *Christians*, it's essential to carefully consider the implications of involvement in *Freemasonry*, fraternities, and sororities and to discern whether participation aligns with their beliefs and convictions. Using biblical figures such as Tubal-Cain and *King Solomon* by *Freemasonry* to create a facade of alignment with Christianity is a deceptive tactic that believers must be wary of, recognizing the fundamental differences between Masonic teachings and the gospel of **Jesus Christ**.

3

**Chapter 3   The Genesis of Prince Hall Freemasonry
& Black Greek Letter Organizations**

"Thou hast set our iniquities before thee, our secret sins in the light of thy countenance." (Psalm 90:8 KJV)

In this chapter, we examine further the origins and development of *Prince Hall Freemasonry and Black Greek Letter Organizations* (*BGLOs*) through the lens of *Christian* principles, shedding light on aspects that conflict with biblical teachings and raise concerns about fidelity to **God**.

1. Prince Hall Freemasonry

- **Origins and Foundation**: *Prince Hall Freemasonry*, named after its founder *Prince Hall*, traces its roots back to the late 18th century. Born into slavery in 1735, *Prince Hall* became a prominent abolitionist and community leader in Boston. Faced with exclusion from mainstream *Freemasonry*, Hall and other *African American* men sought to establish their lodge, which was granted charter status by the *Grand Lodge of England* in 1784. *Prince Hall Freemasonry* was born out of a desire for fellowship and empowerment among *African Americans*. While the organization provided a sense of community in the face of racial discrimination, its foundation on secret rituals and oaths raises questions about its alignment with *Christian* values.

- **Mission and Principles**: *Prince Hall Freemasonry* was founded on the principles of brotherhood, equality, and community service principles. The organization provided *African Americans* with a platform for fellowship, self-improvement, and philanthropy at a time when racial discrimination and segregation were rampant in America. Despite its noble mission of brotherhood and philanthropy, *Prince Hall Freemasonry's* reliance on esoteric symbolism and initiation ceremonies may inadvertently lead members away from a steadfast devotion to **God**. The organization's promotion of a generic "*Supreme Being*" and the swearing of allegiance to Masonic principles above all else is a form of idolatry and a violation of the first commandment.

- **Impact & Legacy**: *Prince Hall Freemasonry* played a pivotal role in the social, political, and economic advancement of *African Americans*. Through its network of lodges, *Prince Hall Masons* provided support and mentorship to their members, fostering a sense of unity and empowerment within the *Black* community. While *Prince Hall Freemasonry* has undoubtedly made significant contributions to the social and economic advancement of *African Americans*, its adherence to rituals and practices that are incompatible with *Christian* beliefs raises concerns about its ultimate allegiance and fidelity to **God**.

2. Black Greek Letter Organizations (*BGLOs*):

- **Emergence and Growth**: *BGLOs* emerged in response to the exclusionary practices of mainstream collegiate fraternities and sororities, offering *African American* students a sense of belonging and support. Some of the founding members of each of the **BGLO** were also members of *Freemasonry*, thus much of its rituals and principles are embedded within them. Their reliance on secret rituals and the promotion of exclusivity within **BGLOs** have led members away from a sole relationship with **God** either blending it or replacing it with the worship of false Greek gods and worldly ideals.

- **Founding Principles**: Each *BGLO* has its unique history and founding principles, but they all share a commitment to scholarship, leadership, and community service. From *Alpha Phi Alpha Fraternity, Inc.*, the first *BGLO* founded at **Cornell University** in 1906, to *Zeta Phi Beta Sorority Inc.*, established at **Howard University** in 1920, these organizations have left an indelible mark on American society. While *BGLOs* espouse scholarship, leadership, and service principles, their rituals and traditions mirror those of mainstream secret societies like *Freemasonry*, raising concerns about their compatibility with *Christian* teachings. The emphasis on secrecy and allegiance to the organization above all else conflicts with the biblical mandate to worship **God** alone and to uphold truth and transparency in all endeavors.

- **Legacy & Influence**: *BGLOs* have undeniably played a significant role in shaping *African American* culture, leadership, and activism. Their initiatives such as voter registration drives, educational scholarships, and community outreach programs, have been instrumental in uplifting and empowering marginalized communities nationwide. However, despite their positive contributions, *BGLOs* must confront the spiritual implications of their practices and rituals. The perpetuation of traditions that promote allegiance to anything other than **God** hinders members from fully embracing their **Christian** faith and living according to its principles.

3. Challenges & Criticisms

- **Internal Struggles**: *Prince Hall Freemasonry* and *BGLOs* face internal challenges and criticisms. Issues such as hazing, elitism, corruption, and gang-like behavior are symptomatic of a broader spiritual malaise that threatens to undermine these organizations' integrity and efficacy. There have been incidents where BGLOs physically fight each other, one organization against another, which further promotes hatred and violence among African Americans towards each other.

- **External Perceptions**: Externally, *Prince Hall Freemasonry* and *BGLOs* are often misunderstood or misrepresented by mainstream society. While they may espouse principles of brotherhood and service, their adherence to rituals and practices that conflict with *Christian* teachings perpetuate a false sense of spiritual fulfillment and lead members astray from the truth of **God's word**. Despite their shortcomings, *Prince Hall Freemasonry* and *BGLOs* continue to wield influence within the *African American* community. However, their ultimate legacy will be determined not by their temporal achievements, but by their fidelity to **God** and adherence to his commandments.

In conclusion, the genesis of *Prince Hall Freemasonry and Black Greek Letter Organizations* represents a complex interplay of social, cultural, and spiritual dynamics. While these organizations have undoubtedly provided a sense of belonging and empowerment to many within the *African American* community, their adherence to rituals and practices that conflict with **Christian** teachings raises significant concerns about their spiritual integrity and fidelity to **God**. As members of these organizations grapple with these issues, they must prayerfully consider their allegiance and seek guidance from *God's* word in all their endeavors.

4

"Be ye not unequally yoked together with unbelievers: for what fellowship hath righteousness with unrighteousness? and what communion hath light with darkness?" (2 Corinthians 6:14 KJV)

In this chapter, we turn to the ultimate authority—the *Bible*—to gain insight into the true nature of secret societies. By examining biblical principles and teachings, we'll uncover the inherent contradictions between secret societies' practices and the **word of God**.

1. Light vs. Darkness

- **Scriptural Foundation**: The *Bible* unequivocally condemns secrecy and hidden agendas, urging believers to walk in the light and expose the deeds of darkness. Scriptures such as *Ephesians 5:11* ("**Have nothing to do with the fruitless deeds of darkness, but rather expose them**") serve as a stark reminder of our responsibility to uphold truth and transparency.

- **Contradictions with Secrecy**: Secret societies thrive on secrecy, shrouding their rituals and practices in darkness. This stands in direct opposition to the biblical mandate to live lives of openness and honesty, free from the deceptive schemes of the enemy.

2. The Dangers of Idolatry

- **Scriptural Warnings**: Idolatry is repeatedly condemned throughout the *Bible* as a grave sin that provokes the jealousy of God. *Exodus 20:3-5* ("*You shall have no other gods before me... You shall not bow down to them or worship them; for I, the Lord your God, am a jealous God*") underscores the seriousness of worshiping false gods or idols.

- **Idolatrous Practices**: Secret societies, with their elaborate rituals and oaths of allegiance, lead members into idolatry by having their joining members perform satanic rituals to obtain membership. This blatant disregard for the first commandment is a clear affront to the sovereignty of *God* and *His* rightful place as the one true object of worship. In God's eyes, these rituals aren't seen as imagery but as an **act of disobedience towards Him**.

3. Fellowship vs. Brotherhood

- **Biblical Fellowship**: The *Bible* emphasizes the importance of fellowship among believers, encouraging mutual support, encouragement, and accountability. *Hebrews 10:24-25* ("*And let us consider how we may spur one another on toward love and good deeds, not giving up meeting together, as some are in the habit of doing, but encouraging one another*") highlights the value of authentic *Christian* community.

- **Counterfeit Brotherhood**: Secret societies offer a counterfeit version of fellowship, luring members with promises of camaraderie and belonging. However, this fellowship is built on a foundation of secrecy and deception, devoid of the genuine love and accountability found within the body of Christ.

4. The Call To Discernment

- **Scriptural Wisdom**: The **Bible** calls believers to exercise discernment and wisdom in all aspects of life. *Proverbs 4:23* ("*Above all else, guard your heart, for everything you do flows from it*") reminds us of the importance of guarding against deception and falsehood.

- **Testing The Spirits**: Believers are urged to test the spirits to discern whether they are from *God* (*1 John 4:1*). This principle applies to all aspects of life, including involvement in secret societies. By aligning their actions with the truth of God's word, believers can safeguard themselves against spiritual compromise.

In conclusion, the *Bible* provides a clear and unequivocal perspective on secret societies. Their practices of secrecy, idolatry, and counterfeit fellowship stand in stark contrast to the principles and teachings found within God's word. As believers, we are called to walk in the light, expose the deeds of darkness, and uphold the truth of God's word in all areas of our lives. By aligning ourselves with biblical principles, we can navigate the dangers of deception and remain steadfast in our faith and devotion to God.

5

"Wherefore, my dearly beloved, flee from idolatry." (*I Corinthians 10:14 KJV*)

The history of idolatry and false religions is as old as humanity itself. From the earliest days after creation, humans have frequently turned away from the worship of the true **God**, choosing instead to create and worship false gods fashioned from their imaginations. This chapter explores the scriptural narratives, historical developments, and God's continuous efforts to call humanity back to Himself. We'll also delve into how Satan has used idolatry as a tool to lead people astray and then accuse them before God because of their sin of idolatry.

Biblical Origins of Idolatry

Garden of Eden: The origin of human disobedience begins in the idyllic setting of **Eden** (**Genesis 3**). Here, Adam and Eve chose to heed the serpent's deceit over God's direct command. This pivotal moment did more than introduce sin; it laid the foundational attitude that leads to idolatry— man's desire to elevate himself and obtain knowledge apart from God's divine instructions.

Cain's Lineage and The Development of Idolatry: The history of idolatry and false religions can be traced back to the early descendants of Adam and Eve, mainly through the divergent paths of their sons, Cain and Seth. This divergence highlights the initial establishment of practices that either drew humanity away from **God** or sought to reconnect with Him. After

Cain was cursed for murdering his brother Abel, he was driven away from the presence of the **Lord** (*Genesis 4:16*). Cain settled in the land of Nod, east of Eden, and his descendants began to establish a society increasingly detached from God. Cain's great-great-grandson Lamech, for instance, not only followed in his ancestor's violent footsteps but also boasted about it (*Genesis 4:23-24*). This lineage is marked by significant advancements in human culture, including the creation of tools and musical instruments by Jubal and Tubal-Cain (*Genesis 4:21-22*). While these advancements themselves weren't inherently idolatrous, they represent humanity's focus on self-sufficiency and cultural development apart from **God**. As Cain's descendants advanced technologically and culturally, there's an implication that these creations could've been used for purposes that led them further from **God**. Instruments of music and tools of bronze and iron, while beneficial, could also become objects of worship or means to support idolatrous practices, emphasizing human achievement over divine dependence. This pattern of self-reliance and deviation from **God** set a precedent for idolatry and false religions.

Seth's Lineage & The Reawakening of Divine Worship: In stark contrast, Seth's lineage is noted for a significant spiritual reawakening. After the birth of Seth's son Enos, it's recorded that "**at that time people began to call on the name of the Lord**" (*Genesis 4:26*). This marks a pivotal return to divine worship, suggesting that Seth's descendants sought to reestablish a relationship with **God** that was neglected or distorted since the time of Adam and Eve. The phrase "**call on the name of the Lord**" signifies more than just prayer; it indicates a deliberate and communal effort to seek and worship **God**. This return to **God** among Seth's descendants can be seen as the foundation for a lineage that would continue to uphold and advance true worship and obedience to **God**, contrasting sharply with the path taken by Cain's descendants.

Implications For Idolatry & True Worship: The divergence between Cain's and Seth's lineages illustrates the fundamental human choice between self-reliance and divine dependence. Cain's descendants, in their achievements, embody the spirit of idolatry by focusing on human innovation and societal development apart from **God**. In contrast, Seth's descendants, beginning with Enos, represent the turning back to God, acknowledging His sovereignty, and seeking His presence. This early narrative sets the stage for the ongoing struggle between idolatry and true worship that permeates human history. It underscores the importance of communal worship and the dangers of self-reliance and cultural achievements becoming ends in themselves, rather than means to glorify **God**. Understanding this divergence helps to frame the broader biblical narrative of humanity's recurring temptation to idolatry and God's relentless call to return to Him.

Tower of Babel: The construction of the *Tower of Babel* (*Genesis 11:1-9*) is another early example of collective human effort to achieve godlike stature without divine sanction. This endeavor wasn't merely about building a city or a tower but represented a significant act of self-idolization and a rejection of divine sovereignty. The scattering of people and the confusion of languages were direct responses to this act, illustrating the disruptive consequences of human pride and rebellion against God's order.

Historical Development of Idol Worship

Ancient Civilizations: The civilizations of *Egypt* and *Babylon* are notable for their intricate systems of gods and goddesses, which permeated every aspect of society from politics to daily routines, influencing *Israel* during its formative years. These pantheons often reflected human attributes, elevating aspects of nature and human personality into divine status. The avoidance of integrating these practices into Israelite life was a significant challenge continually addressed by biblical laws and prophets.

Influence On Israel: Israel's proximity to and interactions with idolatrous nations often led to the adoption of these nations' religious practices, despite explicit prohibitions against such actions in the *Mosaic Law*. The allure of these practices often lay in their tangible rituals and the human-like characteristics of their deities, which were in stark contrast to the abstract, invisible, and monotheistic nature of Yahweh worship.

Israel's Struggle With Idolatry

God's Intentions For Israel: *Israel* was chosen to demonstrate to the world the blessings of living under

God's laws (**Deuteronomy 7:6-8**). Their adherence to God's commandments was supposed to set them apart, illustrating God's wisdom and justice through their prosperity and societal harmony when they obeyed, and their strife and downfall when they didn't. Shortly after the *Exodus*, the Israelites, feeling abandoned by Moses, created and worshiped a golden calf (**Exodus 32**). This incident underlines the persistent vulnerability to idolatry among the Israelites, showcasing their struggle to shift from the tangible idol worship of *Egypt* to the faith-based worship of an unseen God.

During the era of kings, many rulers of *Israel* and *Judah* led the nation into idolatry. *King Solomon's* foreign wives turned his heart towards their gods, and later, *King Ahab* and *Queen Jezebel* aggressively promoted the worship of Baal, directly challenging the worship of *Yahweh*. The prophetic books are replete with examples of prophets challenging these practices and calling the people back to faithfulness to **God**.

The passage from *2 Kings 17:41 KJV*, "*So these nations feared the LORD, and served their graven images, both their children, and their children's children: as did their fathers, so do they unto this day*," provides a profound insight into the persistent and deep-seated issue of divided worship within *Israel*. This dual allegiance reflects the broader theme of idolatry and the struggle to maintain devotion to **God** throughout Israel's history. This scripture comes from a chapter detailing the fall of the northern kingdom of *Israel* to *Assyria*. The Israelites repeatedly violated their covenant with **God** by engaging in idolatrous practices adopted from surrounding nations. Despite the prophetic warnings and divine interventions, Israel's worship became a syncretistic blend of fearing the Lord and serving other gods. The scripture clearly states that while these nations feared the **Lord**, they also served their graven images. This duality is starkly at odds with the fundamental commandment given to Israel "*You shall have no other gods before me*" (*Exodus 20:3*). **God** demanded exclusive worship, as echoed in *Deuteronomy 6:4-5*, "*Hear, O Israel: The Lord our God, the Lord is one. Love the Lord your God with all your heart and with all your soul and with all your strength*."

Implications of Dual Worship: Serving two masters – God and idols – created a significant spiritual and moral compromise. On one hand, the Israelites maintained outward rituals and ceremonies that acknowledged *Yahweh*. On the other hand, they engaged in the worship of graven images, which represented the deities of neighboring cultures, including Baal and Asherah. This dual worship led to a diluted and ineffective faith that wasn't fully committed to the **Lord**. **Jesus** addressed the impossibility of serving two masters in *Matthew 6:24*, stating, "*No one can serve two masters. Either you will hate the one and love the other, or you will be devoted to the one and despise the other*." This principle highlights the inherent conflict in trying to divide one's loyalty. True worship of **God** requires total devotion, which cannot coexist with the veneration of idols.

Intergenerational Impact: The passage from *2 Kings* also mentions that this divided worship was passed down through generations: "*both their children and* *their children's children: as did their fathers, so do they unto this day*." This points to the powerful influence of parental and societal examples on future generations. The failure to only worship **God** not only affected those who initially engaged in idolatry but also entrenched these practices in the cultural and spiritual fabric of the community. This generational continuation of idolatry underscores spiritual compromise's persistent and pervasive nature. It reflects the warning given in **Exodus 20:5**, where God declares that He is "*a jealous God, punishing the children for the sin of the parents to the third and fourth generation of those who hate me*." The consequences of divided worship weren't merely individual but communal, affecting the entire nation of Israel. Throughout Israel's history, God responded to this dual allegiance with calls for repentance through His prophets. *Prophets* like Elijah, Hosea, and Jeremiah condemned idolatry and urged the people to return to only worshipping *Yahweh*. Elijah's challenge on *Mount Carmel* (**1 Kings 18:21**) epitomizes this call "*How long will you waver between two opinions? If the Lord is God, follow him; but if Baal is God, follow him*." Despite these warnings, Israel's repeated failure to abandon idolatry ultimately led to their downfall and exile. However, God's enduring message through the prophets was one of hope and restoration for those who would repent and return to Him with undivided hearts.

Satan's Role In Promoting Idolatry

Satan's tactics have historically involved the cunning distortion of truth and the relentless promotion of spiritual untruths. One of his most insidious strategies is the deliberate blending of the profane with the holy, the good with evil, and the unclean with the clean. This mixing creates a confusing and deceptive environment where it becomes challenging to distinguish between what is true of **God** and what's a cleverly disguised lie. By introducing idol worship, Satan offers humanity a false sense of autonomy from **God**. This appeal to human ego and desires exploits our inherent weaknesses and pride, leading us away from divine truth and towards spiritual decay. The allure of idol worship and false religion is powerful because it provides a seemingly easier path that gratifies immediate desires while subtly undermining our relationship with the true source of life. In the next chapter, I will delve deeper into Satan's nature, exploring how he systematically orchestrates these deceptions to ensnare humanity and separate us from **God**.

Impact of Idolatry On Societies

The worship of idols often involved practices that were morally reprehensible and profoundly destructive. One of the most egregious examples is the worship of Molech, which required child sacrifices. This horrific practice, described in passages *Leviticus 18:21* and *Jeremiah 32:35*, entails parents sacrificing their children by fire, an act that epitomizes the moral depravity idolatry could induce. Similarly, the worship of Ashtoreth (or Asherah) involved temple prostitution, where sexual acts were performed as part of religious rituals. These acts, condemned in passages like *Deuteronomy 23:17* and *1 Kings 14:23-24*, not only corrupted the worshipers but also degraded societal morals by promoting sexual immorality under the guise of religious observance. Other ancient practices included self-mutilation and bloodletting, as seen in the worship of Baal. During the contest on *Mount Carmel*, the prophets of Baal slashed themselves with swords and spears until their blood flowed, hoping to elicit a response from their god (*1 Kings 18:28*). These extreme acts of devotion underscore how idolatry could drive people to self-harm and fanaticism.

Today, modern forms of idolatry manifest through excessive adoration of wealth, fame, and material possessions. While less overt than ancient idol worship, these practices similarly divert devotion and reliance away from **God**. The pursuit of material wealth often becomes a consuming priority, as warned against in *1 Timothy 6:10*, which states "***The love of money is the root of all kinds of evil***." Fame and celebrity culture can create idols out of human beings, shifting focus and admiration away from **God**, as highlighted in **Romans 1:25**, where people "***exchanged the truth about God for a lie, and worshiped and served created things rather than the Creator***." The historical excursion into idolatry and false religions underscores not just human frailty but also God's persistent efforts to guide humanity back to true worship. Through understanding this history, believers can more deeply appreciate their roles in upholding the truths of their faith. By recognizing the subtle forms of modern idolatry and remaining vigilant against spiritual deception, Christians can live lives that glorify **God**. The scriptures serve as both a warning and a guide, reminding us of the importance of devotion to **God** and the dangers of allowing anything to take His rightful place in our hearts. This journey through history is not merely an academic exercise but a spiritual imperative to stay true to the faith and to the God who has continuously called His people back to Himself

"There is a way that seemeth right unto a man, But the end thereof are the ways of death."

Proverbs 16:25 KJV

#BeNotDeceived

6

Chapter 6   *Satan, the Architect of Secret Societies*

"Thou art the anointed cherub that covereth; and I have set thee so: thou wast upon the holy mountain of God; thou hast walked up and down in the midst of the stones of fire. Thou wast perfect in thy ways from the day that thou wast created, till iniquity was found in thee." (Ezekiel 28:14-15 KJV)

Satan's role as the master deceiver is intricately detailed throughout scripture, portraying him as the architect behind the secretive and misleading structures that lead humanity away from **God**. His strategies, built on lies and deception, are fundamental traits that permeate his influence across ages and are vividly reflected in the operations of secret societies.

Father of Lies

Jesus explicitly describes Satan's nature in **John 8:44**, stating, "*You belong to your father, the devil, and you want to carry out your father's desires. He was a murderer from the beginning, not holding to the truth, for there is no truth in him. When he lies, he speaks his native language, for he is a liar and the father of lies.*" This profound declaration underscores Satan's fundamental nature as the ultimate deceiver and manipulator, whose very essence is rooted in falsehood and destruction.

Satan's influence is strikingly evident in the operations of secret societies, which often employ secrecy and coded language to obscure their true practices and beliefs. This deception is a direct reflection of Satan's deceitful nature. Just as Satan twists and distorts the truth to lead people astray, these societies promise enlightenment and hidden knowledge but often entangle their members in deeper confusion and moral compromise. The allure of hidden wisdom and insight mirrors Satan's original deception in the *Garden of Eden*, where he promised Eve that eating the forbidden fruit would open her eyes and make her like **God**, knowing good and evil (***Genesis 3:4-5***). However, this promise led to sin, shame, and separation from God. Secret societies, much like Satan, present an appealing façade. They often cloak their activities in a veneer of respectability, suggesting their rituals and teachings offer profound truths and greater understanding. However, the reality is, that these practices frequently run counter to biblical teachings and lead to spiritual and moral decay. Satan, the father of lies, is adept at crafting these illusions, making falsehoods appear as truths and vice versa. His goal is to keep individuals ensnared in a web of deceit, far removed from the clarity and freedom offered by God's truth.

In addition to promoting secrecy, these societies often engage in morally ambiguous or outright unethical practices under the guise of achieving a greater good or spiritual enlightenment. This mirrors Satan's tactic of presenting sin as beneficial or harmless. In *2 Corinthians 11:14*, Paul warns that "***Satan himself masquerades as an angel of light***." This ability to disguise evil as good is a hallmark of Satan's deceptive strategies and is evident in the operations of many secret societies. These scriptural insights collectively establish Satan as a being whose purpose is rooted in the foundational lies and deceptions that give rise to systems like secret societies. Secret societies often operate under veils of secrecy and purported wisdom, which align perfectly with Satan's methods of obscuring truth and promoting rebellion against **God**. His blueprint for these societies is clear: to weave complex lies and create secretive networks that oppose the simplicity and openness of the gospel.

God of This World

Satan is often referred to as the "*god of this world*," a title that highlights his significant influence over worldly systems and institutions. In **2 Corinthians 4:4**, Paul writes, "***The god of this world has blinded the minds of unbelievers, so that they cannot see the light of the gospel that displays the glory of Christ, who is the image of God***." This scripture underscores Satan's role in blinding humanity to divine truth, embedding ungodly principles within various aspects of society, and perpetuating spiritual darkness.

Many of the world's leaders are or have been, associated with secret societies that often operate under a veil of secrecy and elitism. These organizations, such as the *Freemasons*, *The Illuminati*, and *The Skull and Bones Society*, have been linked to significant political and economic power. For example, several *U.S. Presidents*, including *George Washington*, *Franklin D. Roosevelt*, and *George H.W. Bush*, were known as *Freemasons*. The secrecy and rituals associated with these groups often contradict *Christian* principles, promoting a form of allegiance and loyalty that can rival devotion to **God**.

Satan's influence extends beyond individuals to the very systems and institutions that govern our world. This influence is evident in various aspects of modern culture, including entertainment, education, and politics, where ungodly values are often promoted. The pervasive presence of violence, sexual immorality, and materialism in media, the secularization of educational curricula, and policies that contradict biblical principles are all reflections of this influence.

Pledging allegiance to a flag, while often seen as a patriotic act, can also be viewed as a form of idolatry. Idolatry is not limited to the worship of graven images but extends to any act of placing something or someone above **God** in our lives. The act of pledging allegiance, especially if it involves unconditional loyalty to a nation or its symbols, can conflict with the biblical mandate to have no other gods before the **one true God** (*Exodus 20:3*). **Jesus** clearly distinguished His kingdom from worldly kingdoms in *John 18:36*, "*My kingdom is not of this world: if my kingdom were of this world, then would my servants fight, that I should not be delivered to the Jews: but now is my kingdom not from hence.*" This statement emphasizes that the kingdom of **God** operates on fundamental principles different principles from those of earthly kingdoms. It's not about power, control, or political dominance but about righteousness, peace, and the transformative power of God's love. In stark contrast, Satan's kingdom is very much of this world, as illustrated *in Luke 4:5-6*: "*And the devil, taking him up into an high mountain, shewed unto him all the kingdoms of the world in a moment of time. And the devil said unto him, All this power will I give thee, and the glory of them: for that is delivered* *unto me; and to whomsoever I will I give it.*" Notice in this temptation of **Jesus**, that he never denies what Satan states because what Satan said was true. This passage underscores Satan's permitted authority under **God** but over worldly kingdoms and his capacity to influence earthly leaders and structures. His offer to **Jesus** reflects his control over the political and economic powers of the world, which he uses to propagate his agenda. Satan has skillfully embedded ungodly values and practices within many aspects of society. The normalization of sin through media, the promotion of selfish ambition and greed in business, and the acceptance of moral relativism in education are just a few examples of how Satan's influence permeates the world. These ungodly influences lead people away from **God** and toward spiritual decay.

Global Deceiver

Revelation 12:9 underscores Satan's role as the deceiver of the whole world, stating, "***The great dragon was hurled down—that ancient serpent called the devil, or Satan, who leads the whole world astray. He was hurled to the earth, and his angels with him***." This passage highlights Satan's pervasive influence as the ultimate deceiver, orchestrating a grand scheme to mislead humanity on a global scale. His tactics of deception and manipulation are particularly evident in the operations of secret societies, which mirror his ability to create a unified yet profoundly misleading worldview that directly competes with the global message of the gospel.

Secret societies often operate across continents, recruiting members from diverse cultural and social backgrounds into an intricate web of influence. This widespread reach allows them to promote their teachings and philosophies, which frequently stand in stark contrast to the principles of *Christianity*. By offering promises of hidden knowledge, power, and enlightenment, these organizations captivate individuals who are searching for deeper meaning and purpose, much like Satan lures humanity with false promises and deceitful allurements. His strategy of leading the whole world astray is reflected in the way secret societies cultivate a global network of adherents who are bound by shared rituals, symbols, and oaths. This network creates a sense of unity and belonging among members, drawing them away from the inclusive and redemptive message of the gospel. Instead of promoting the truth of **God's word**, secret societies often disseminate teachings that are designed to elevate human wisdom and knowledge above God's commandments, aligning with Satan's original lie in the *Garden of Eden* ***"For all that is in the world—the desires of the flesh and the desires of the eyes and pride of life—is not from the Father but is from the world"*** (***1 John 2:16***). Satan's influence through secret societies also manifests in their promotion of a worldview that's often antithetical to the gospel. The gospel calls for self-sacrifice, love, and service to others (***Mark 10:45***), while secret societies frequently emphasize self-improvement, personal power, and the attainment of hidden knowledge. This divergence creates a spiritual dichotomy, where the principles of these societies directly oppose the teachings of **Christ**. In ***Matthew 7:15***, **Jesus** warns, ***"Beware of false*** *prophets, who come to you in sheep's clothing but inwardly are ravenous wolves.*" Secret societies, with their alluring promises and hidden truths, can be seen as modern-day embodiments of this warning, presenting themselves as harmless or even beneficial while leading people away from the true gospel. Promoting a worldview that elevates human wisdom and knowledge above divine revelation contributes to a cultural shift away from biblical truth. This shift can be seen in various aspects of society, from the normalization of occult practices in media and entertainment to the acceptance of relativistic moral standards in education and politics. The global influence of secret societies is a testament to Satan's ability to weave a complex web of deceit that spans cultures and nations, drawing countless individuals away from the saving knowledge of *Jesus Christ*.

Prince of Disobedience

Ephesians 2:2 labels Satan as the "*prince of the power of the air, the spirit who now works in the sons of disobedience.*" This depiction highlights his pervasive influence over those who rebel against God's commands. This sinister influence is notably apparent in the operations of secret societies, which cultivate a culture steeped in exclusivity and hierarchical structures grounded on esoteric knowledge and arcane rituals. These societies' practices, often shrouded in secrecy and accessible only to a select few, starkly contrast with the Biblical mandate for transparency and humility in worship and community life. The doctrines and rituals of these groups frequently challenge or outright contradict the core teachings of scripture. For instance, the rituals might involve oaths of secrecy that bind members to the society above all else, directly opposing **Jesus'** call to *"seek first the kingdom of God and His righteousness"* (**Matthew 6:33**). Secret societies often employ symbols that carry hidden meanings, creating an illusion of alternative secret knowledge that's only accessible to the initiated. Moreover, the hierarchical and elitist structures of secret societies echo Satan's pride and desire for power. *Isaiah 14:12-14* depicts Satan's fall from heaven due to his ambition to ascend above the stars of **God** and become like the *Most High*. Similarly, secret societies often create stratified systems where members must ascend through various levels or degrees, each promising greater knowledge and power. This pursuit of elevation and secret wisdom fosters an environment of pride, directly opposing the humility and openness that characterize true **Christian** fellowship. Additionally, the secretive activities often associated with these groups can include morally ambiguous or unethical behaviors justified under the guise of achieving a greater good or accessing higher spiritual enlightenment. This directly contravenes the biblical instruction to live lives marked by clear moral integrity and openness (**Philippians 2:15**). The *Apostle Paul* warns against such behaviors, advising Christians to *"have nothing to do with the fruitless deeds of darkness, but rather expose them"* (**Ephesians 5:11**). Secret societies' emphasis on hidden knowledge and private rituals exemplifies the workings of the "prince of the power of the air" in fostering disobedience among the sons and daughters of humanity. This disobedience is not merely about breaking divine laws but involves a fundamental breach of the relational and transparent way of life that **God** desires for His people. The secrecy and elitism promoted by these societies serve to isolate their members from the broader community, often leading to a dual life where the values professed publicly differ greatly from those practiced privately.

Adversary To Righteousness

In *Acts 13:10*, where Paul confronts Elymas, the sorcerer for opposing the truths of the gospel, we see a confrontation with the kind of opposition that Satan orchestrates. Secret societies can be seen as modern-day Elymases, who subtly oppose the spread of the gospel by promoting alternative spiritualities and loyalties that stand in direct opposition to the message of **Christ**. These organizations often present themselves as benevolent and wise, promising enlightenment, self-improvement, and secret knowledge. They appeal to the innate human desire for belonging, significance, and deeper understanding. However, beneath this attractive veneer lies a profound spiritual danger. Just as Elymas, the sorcerer, tried to turn people away from the faith, secret societies propagate teachings that lead their members away from the truth of the gospel. Moreover, the commitment these societies demand often requires members to prioritize their allegiance to the group over their commitment to **Christ**. This can lead to a conflict of interest where the teachings and demands of the society contradict biblical principles. In opposition to the gospel, secret societies also tend to create an environment of moral ambiguity. They often promote relativistic ethical standards that stand in stark contrast to the absolute moral truths presented in scripture. This moral flexibility can lead members to justify behaviors and beliefs that are incompatible with Christian teachings. The result is a gradual erosion of biblical values and a growing acceptance of practices that are antithetical to the faith. Seeing the role of secret societies as modern-day Elymases helps believers recognize the subtle yet pervasive influence of Satan's deceptions.

Conclusion

Recognizing Satan as the architect of secret societies equips believers with the critical knowledge needed to identify and combat these dark influences. Each of Satan's attributes—liar, deceiver, promoter of disobedience, and opposer of the gospel—manifests in the characteristics and activities of secret societies. These groups, with their secretive operations, elitist structures, alternative spiritual philosophies, and global influence, epitomize the deceptive, divisive, and destructive strategies of their architect, Satan. Recognizing this alignment highlights the importance of vigilance and strict adherence to the truth of scripture in a world where the father of lies continually seeks to ensnare and deceive.

Choose!

Both, is not an option. (Joshua 24:15)

#BeNotDeceived

Quote by Tommy Arbuckie

7

Chapter 7 Unveiling The Idolatrous & False Religious Nature of Secret Societies

"Wherefore, my dearly beloved, flee from idolatry" (*I Corinthians 10:14 KJV*)

In this chapter, we embark on a journey to uncover the disturbing reality of secret societies, exposing their hidden agenda of idolatry and false religion. We'll navigate through the evidence, shining a light on the stark reality that these clandestine organizations are, indeed, conduits of satanic influence and idolatrous practices. By critically examining their rituals and practices, we'll reveal the insidious influence, leading members down a path of spiritual deception and betrayal.

Exposing The Deceptive Rituals

Veiled in Darkness: Within the cloaked chambers of secret societies lie rituals and symbolism that hint at a darker truth. Secret societies cloak their rituals in secrecy and mystique, drawing members into a web of deception from which escape becomes increasingly difficult. Behind closed doors, initiates are subjected to sinister ceremonies that blur the lines between enlightenment and spiritual bondage. The intricate symbolism and elaborate initiation ceremonies serve as a guise for the covert indoctrination into practices that are synonymous with witchcraft and satanic rituals.

Unmasking Deception: The symbolism employed by secret societies often serves as a guise for their true intentions. From ancient *Egyptian* motifs to occult imagery, these symbols betray a hidden agenda rooted in the worship of false gods and satanic forces. Despite attempts to justify their rituals as mere tradition or philosophical exploration, the underlying motives become apparent upon closer inspection. The allure of mystique and exclusivity conceals the sinister agenda of leading members down a path of spiritual corruption and idolatrous worship.

Unmasking The Idolatrous Practices

Oaths and Pledges of Allegiance: Central to the workings of secret societies are the binding oaths of allegiance, sworn upon penalty of severe consequences. Members of secret societies are required to pledge allegiance to the organization above all else, swearing oaths that bind them to a false religion. The practice of pledging allegiance without prior knowledge of the oath is one of the reasons why these organizations are termed secret societies. It remains a secret what commitments you'll be making; you're not allowed to review the oath beforehand and are instructed to repeat the words as they're told to you or simply say "**I do**" after words are spoken. These oaths, often accompanied by gruesome penalties for betrayal, elevate the society to a position of reverence that rivals that of **God** Himself. Examples include *Freemasonry's Entered Apprentice Oath*, which binds the initiate under penalty of having their throat slit, and the solemn pledge to prioritize the interests of the fraternity over all else. Such acts of devotion to the organization elevate it to a position of reverence and adoration, effectively usurping the rightful place of God in the hearts of its members.

Worship of False Idols: Through their rituals and practices, secret societies lead members into idolatry, worshiping false gods and demonic forces. Members are ensnared in a web of deceit, bowing down before false idols crafted from the fabric of secrecy and deception. The act of pledging loyalty to an earthly entity, accompanied by rituals that instill fear and subservience, is nothing short of idolatry in its purest form. From the veneration of ancient deities to the invocation of occult powers, these practices betray a blatant disregard for the one true **God**.

Unraveling Historical & Cultural Contexts

A Legacy of Darkness: Throughout history, secret societies have left a trail of darkness and intrigue, their existence shrouded in mystery and suspicion. From the pagan mystery cults of ancient Greece to the modern-day *Freemasons*, the patterns of idolatry and false religion persist, ensnaring countless souls in their web of deceit. From ancient cults to modern-day fraternities, the patterns of idolatry and satanic influence persist, leaving an indelible mark on the fabric of society.

A Global Epidemic: Secret societies are a global phenomenon, infiltrating every corner of the world with their poisonous doctrines. Across diverse cultures and regions, the insidious tendrils of secret societies have taken root, exploiting mankind's vulnerabilities for their nefarious ends. What may appear as a harmless tradition in one culture is, in reality, a gateway to spiritual bondage and enslavement, a tool of Satan to lead humanity astray from the path of righteousness.

A Call To Repentance & Redemption

Heeding The Warning Signs: In the face of such pervasive darkness, individuals must heed the warning signs and reject the false promises of secret societies standing firm in their faith and discernment. The seductive allure of secret societies must be met with unwavering resolve and steadfast faith in God. The promise of worldly power and prestige at the cost of offending God is nothing short of a ticket to eternal damnation.

Seeking Redemption: For those ensnared in the web of secret societies, there is hope for redemption and salvation. By rejecting the siren song of secrecy and embracing the truth of God's word, individuals can break free from the shackles of idolatry and satanic influence. Turning away from false gods and embracing the one true **God**, individuals can break free from the shackles of idolatry and find true spiritual fulfillment in His divine grace. It's only through unwavering faith and devotion to the one true **God** that salvation and redemption can be found.

In conclusion, the evidence is overwhelming: secret societies are bastions of idolatry and false religion, leading countless souls down a path of spiritual destruction. It's incumbent upon all who seek truth and righteousness to heed the warning signs and turn away from the path of deception, exposing these dark forces for what they truly are and to stand firm in their faith in God. Only through repentance and redemption can we hope to break free from the clutches of darkness and find true salvation in His divine grace.

8

"Take heed to thyself, lest thou make a covenant with the inhabitants of the land whither thou goest, lest it be for a snare in the midst of thee: But ye shall destroy their altars, break their images, and cut down their groves: For thou shalt worship no other god: for the LORD, whose name is Jealous, is a jealous God: Lest thou make a covenant with the inhabitants of the land, and they go a whoring after their gods, and do sacrifice unto their gods" (Exodus 34:12-15 KJV)

In this chapter, we'll explore the concepts of altars, rituals, oaths, and covenants. These elements are foundational in many secret societies and have profound spiritual implications. The use of altars to perform rituals and the use of oaths to make a covenant isn't evil within themselves. However, by understanding their definitions and examining biblical examples, we can discern how their misuse leads to practices that are contrary to God's will for our lives.

1. Altars

Definition: An altar is a structure used for the presentation of religious offerings, sacrifices, or other ritualistic purposes. This structure can be as simple as a table, platform, or stone, or as an elaborate display made from marble, wood, masonry, etc.

Altars are found at shrines, temples, churches, and other places of worship by non-Christians and Christians. They're central in many religious practices as places of worship and communion with the divine.

Biblical Examples

●**Noah's Altar**: After the flood, Noah built an altar to the Lord and offered burnt offerings, which pleased God (*Genesis 8:20-21*).

●**Abraham's Altar**: Abraham built an altar to God when he was called to leave his home and journey to a new land (*Genesis 12:7*).

●**Children of Israel Altar**: God gave specific instructions for how altars were to be built by them for Him. (*Exodus 20:22-26*)

Use In Secret Societies

In secret societies, altars are often used in initiation ceremonies and other rituals. These altars may be dedicated to various deities or symbolic representations that aren't aligned with the God of the Bible. For example, *Masonic* rituals often involve altars where oaths and vows are made, invoking various figures and symbols.

While altars themselves aren't evil, their use in worshiping false gods or in ungodly rituals is detestable to God. The **Bible** consistently condemns the construction of altars to other gods, emphasizing that worship should be directed only to the one true **God** (*Exodus 20:3-5*). The presence of an altar during any ritual denotes that a spiritual event is taking place. You must ask yourself these questions if an altar is present during a ritual in which you're participating. To whom was the altar erected? What is the name of the deity? What is the purpose of the altar at the time of use? Answering these questions will generally point you in the direction of if this event is pleasing to **God**. In addition, don't think God is pleased with what's happening because a **Bible** is present or someone prays to God during the event, that God is pleased with what's happening. This may not be the case especially if the altar was set up for other gods. **Be not deceived**!

2. Rituals

Definition: A ritual is a set of actions performed according to a prescribed order, often imbued with symbolic meaning and conducted as part of a religious or cultural ceremony.

Rituals serve as a means to express and reinforce beliefs, values, and traditions within a community. Rituals can range from daily practices like prayer and meditation to elaborate ceremonies marking significant life events such as baptisms, weddings, and funerals. In a religious context, rituals are seen as acts of worship, devotion, and communion with the divine, often aimed at invoking blessings, seeking forgiveness, or commemorating sacred events. Rituals help to create a sense of order, structure, and continuity within a community, linking individuals to their collective history and shared identity. They can also provide comfort, stability, and a sense of belonging, particularly during times of change or uncertainty. However, when rituals are detached from their original spiritual or moral foundations, they can become mere formalities, losing their intended significance and potentially leading to empty or misguided practices.

Biblical Examples

•**God's covenant with Abraham**: The covenant is solemnized through a ritual involving animal sacrifices. (*Genesis 15:9-10*)

•**Passover**: The Passover is a ritual commanded by God to commemorate the Israelites' deliverance from Egypt (*Exodus 12:14*).

•**Baptism**: In the *New Testament*, baptism is a ritual symbolizing repentance and acceptance of **Jesus Christ** (*Matthew 28:19*).

Use In Secret Societies

Secret societies are known for their elaborate rituals, which often involve symbolic actions, recitations, and ceremonial attire. These rituals are designed to impart esoteric knowledge and bind members together in shared and often secretive experiences.

While rituals in themselves aren't inherently evil, their purpose and the values they promote are crucial in determining their alignment with God's will and teachings. Rituals can be significant in religious practice. The use of rituals in secret societies often involves elements that are contrary to *Christian* teachings. For instance, rituals that invoke deities or spirits other than God, or involve secret knowledge not revealed in scripture, can lead participants away from true faith. These types of satanic rituals often involve the lighting of candles in the spirit of the organization or the name of the organization which shouldn't be taken lightly.

3. Oaths

Definition: An oath is a solemn promise, often invoking a divine witness, regarding one's future action or behavior.

An oath is a commitment that's verbally stated by a person. An oath refers to a promise being made to another person calling upon God to be a witness of the said promise. Performing an oath shouldn't be taken lightly, as God himself will judge you accordingly if you fail to keep it.

Biblical Examples

•**God's Oath to Abraham**: God makes an oath to Abraham regarding his offspring. (*Genesis 15:5*). *Hebrew 6:13* states when God made this promise to Abraham because He could swear by no greater, he sware by himself.

•**Abraham's Oath**: Abraham made his servant swear an oath to find a wife for Isaac from his relatives, not from the Canaanites (*Genesis 24:3*).

●**Jesus on Oaths**: **Jesus** taught not to swear at all but to let one's yes be yes and no be no (***Matthew 5:34-37***).

Use In Secret Societies

Secret societies often require members to take oaths that pledge secrecy and loyalty to the organization above all else. These oaths can include severe penalties for breaking them, such as the infamous *Masonic* oaths that include graphic threats of punishment for disobedience. Secret societies don't allow a person to review the words they'll take as an oath; this deceitful practice binds individuals to words and actions they're not fully made aware of until it's too late. All potential members are simply told to repeat the words being stated to them or say "**I do**" to affirm what's being asked of them as they're going through the ritual. This behavior further highlights how dangerous it is to join a secret society.

Oaths aren't inherently evil, but when they demand loyalty that supersedes one's allegiance to **God**, they become problematic. The **Bible** teaches that our ultimate allegiance must be to **God** alone, and any oath that contradicts this isn't pleasing to Him. Similarly, an oath taken to another god can also produce a curse in your life as **God** sees this as idolatry.

4. Covenants

Definition: A covenant, in its biblical context, isn't just a promise, but a formal, legal, and binding agreement between two or more parties, often involving mutual commitments and responsibilities. A covenant that's formed when oaths are taken is not to be taken lightly, as it carries the weight of legal and moral obligations.

In the rich tapestry of the biblical narrative, covenants stand as pivotal threads, representing binding commitments made between God and humanity or between individuals under God's authority. These agreements with their roots in ancient history, reveal God's relational nature and His desire for faithful obedient people. They serve as the framework through which God interacts with humanity encompassing promises of blessings for obedience and consequences for disobedience, reflecting God's justice and mercy.

Biblical Examples

●**God's Covenant with Abraham**: God made a covenant with Abraham, promising to make him a great nation and to bless all nations through his descendants (*Genesis 12:1-3*).

●**New Covenant in Christ: Jesus** established the new covenant through His death and resurrection, offering salvation to all who believe in Him (*Luke 22:20*).

Use In Secret Societies

Covenants in secret societies often involve binding agreements between members, promising mutual support and adherence to the society's rules and secrets. These covenants, while fostering a sense of community, can sometimes demand loyalty that conflicts with one's faith commitments, thereby raising urgent ethical considerations and the need for discernment. From a biblical perspective, covenants aren't to be taken lightly. They're sacred and reflect God's will and purposes. Covenants that bind individuals to practices or beliefs contrary to scripture are not in line with God's intentions. The **Bible** cautions against making covenants with those who don't follow God's ways, as this can lead to spiritual compromise (*Exodus 23:32*).

In everyday life, covenants are not to be taken lightly. They can be found in various forms such as marriage vows, business contracts, and personal commitments, emphasizing trust, fidelity, and mutual responsibility. However, when covenants are made with ungodly intentions or in contradiction to God's commands, they can lead to spiritual bondage and moral compromise. This is particularly evident in the context of secret societies, where members might take oaths or enter into covenants that conflict with their primary allegiance to God, leading to a dangerous duality in their spiritual lives. Covenants aren't merely casual agreements; they're legal and binding commitments that require formal actions to dissolve. When entered into, they establish obligations that must be honored, and simply walking away from them is insufficient to nullify their effects. **Jesus** highlights the binding nature of agreements in *Matthew 18:18*, stating, "*Truly I tell you, whatever you bind on earth will be bound in heaven, and whatever you loose on earth will be loosed in heaven*." This underscores the spiritual and legal weight of covenants, affirming they have consequences in the earthly and heavenly realms. For instance, in marriage, a covenant is established between the spouses before God and witnesses. To dissolve this covenant, a formal process of divorce is required, reflecting the serious nature of the commitment made (**Matthew 19:6**). Similarly, when individuals enter into covenants within secret societies or other organizations, they must formally renounce and break these agreements to be fully released from their binding terms and any associated spiritual implications. This process of renunciation is essential to ensure that all ties are severed and the individual is freed from any lingering obligations or influences, underscoring the gravity and seriousness of covenants in our lives.

The Covenant Between Jacob & Laban

Next, I want to review the story of the covenant between Jacob and Laban. After this story and the next one I'll break down each stage (ritual oath and covenant) they went through to establish their covenants. This will give us more insight into how evil intentions can be mixed with good when covenants are established. *Genesis 31* provides a comprehensive example of how altars, oaths, rituals, and covenants were integral to establishing agreements and relationships in biblical times. This narrative highlights the solemnity and binding nature of such agreements, often invoking the divine as witnesses to their commitments.

A. The Ritual

The setting up of a stone pillar and a heap of stones, called Galeed, along with the sacrificial meal that follows, are ritual acts that signify the solemnization of their agreement. These rituals serve as tangible symbols of their covenant, marking the place and moment of their agreement.

•*Genesis 31:46-54 Jacob said to his kinsmen, "Gather stones. "So they took stones and made a heap, and they ate there by the heap."* This heap is a witness between us today. Therefore, it was named Galeed, and also Mizpah, because he said, *"May the Lord keep watch between you and me when we are away from each other."*

This gathering around a meal serves as a communal acknowledgment of their newly established peace. It's a typical ancient Near Eastern ritual to confirm a covenant, involving not only the primary parties but also their extended families and communities.

B. Oath

The covenant between Jacob and Laban is solidified by mutual oaths taken in the name of their respective deities. Laban swears by both the God of Abraham and the God of Nahor, thereby invoking a false god alongside the true **God**. This dual invocation highlights the mixture of true and false worship present in Laban's practice. In contrast, Jacob distinctly chooses to swear only by the *"Fear of his father Isaac,"* demonstrating his exclusive allegiance to the true **God**.

•*Genesis 31:53* "*May the God of Abraham and the God of Nahor, the God of their father, judge between us." So Jacob swore by the fear of his father Isaac*.

The presence of God as a witness to an oath should profoundly affect our attitude toward agreements. It reminds us that our commitments aren't only before men but also before God, who sees and judges our intentions and actions. This reverence should compel us to uphold our promises with integrity and faithfulness, recognizing we're accountable to the one true **God**. The distinction Jacob makes in swearing by the **fear** of Isaac underscores the importance of maintaining purity in our oaths and commitments, avoiding any association with false deities or compromised worship.

C. Covenant

After a tense pursuit and confrontation, Jacob and Laban agree to make a covenant, marking it with a heap of stones. This covenant serves to establish boundaries and peaceful relations between them, preventing future hostilities and ensuring mutual respect.

●*Genesis 31:44-45 "Come now, let us make a covenant, you and I, and let it serve as a witness between us." So Jacob took a stone and set it up as a pillar."*

The covenant marks a significant turning point in their relationship, transforming a potentially volatile situation into one of mutual respect and peaceful coexistence. It underscores the power of covenants to bring resolution and harmony where there was previously discord. This narrative vividly illustrates how altars, oaths, rituals, and covenants are interwoven to establish solemn and binding agreements. The biblical context shows while these practices aren't inherently evil, their purpose and the deities invoked are crucial in determining their alignment with God's will. The use of these elements in a manner that honors God can lead to peace and reconciliation, as seen in the story of Jacob and Laban.

Isaac's Covenant With Abimelech

Another profound example of the use of altars, oaths, rituals, and covenants can be found in the story of Isaac's covenant with Abimelech in **Genesis 26**. This narrative highlights how people are drawn to make covenants with those who display God's favor and integrity, often witnessing the good in them and seeking alliances for various motives which we need to consider the reason why.

A. <u>Ritual</u>

The ritual involved in this covenant includes a feast prepared by Isaac, symbolizing their agreement and the establishment of peaceful relations.

●*Genesis 26:30 "Isaac then made a feast for them, and they ate and drank."*

This communal meal serves as a ritual act that solemnizes their agreement, reflecting the ancient Near Eastern tradition of marking covenants with shared meals.

B. Oath

When Abimelech, the King of the Philistines, saw that **God** was with Isaac, he sought to make a covenant of peace with him. This covenant was solidified by mutual oaths, demonstrating the seriousness and binding nature of their agreement.

●*Genesis 26:28-29 "They answered, 'We saw clearly that the Lord was with you; so we said, There ought to be a sworn agreement between us—between us and you. Let us make a treaty with you that you will do us no harm, just as we did not harm you but always treated you well and sent you away peacefully. And now you are blessed by the Lord.'"*

The recognition of God's presence with Isaac compelled Abimelech to seek a formal oath, ensuring peaceful relations and mutual respect.

C. Covenant

The covenant between Isaac and Abimelech was established to ensure peace and mutual benefit. It acknowledged God's blessing on Isaac and sought to create a formal agreement that would prevent future conflicts.

●*Genesis 26:31 "Early the next morning the men swore an oath to each other. Then Isaac sent them on their way, and they went away peacefully."*

This covenant not only established peace between Isaac and Abimelech but also highlighted the recognition of God's hand upon Isaac's life, prompting others to seek alliances with him. This narrative illustrates how those who witness the good in God's people and His blessings upon them are often drawn to make covenants with them. This dynamic can also be observed in modern contexts, where secret societies and organizations seek out the best and brightest individuals, recognizing their potential and the value they bring. This is similar to what happened in *Daniel 1:3-4, 6-7*, where *King Nebuchadnezzar* sought young men from Israel who were knowledgeable and competent to serve in his palace. These organizations often use the good in God's children for their purposes, much like how Nebuchadnezzar aimed to utilize the talents of Daniel and his friends.

•*Daniel 1:3-4* "*Then the king ordered Ashpenaz, chief of his court officials, to bring into the king's service some of the Israelites from the royal family and the nobility—young men without any physical defect, handsome, showing aptitude for every kind of learning, well informed, quick to understand, and qualified to serve in the king's palace.*"

•*Daniel 1:6-7* "*Among those who were chosen were some from Judah: Daniel, Hananiah, Mishael, and Azariah. The chief official gave them new names: to Daniel, the name Belteshazzar; to Hananiah, Shadrach; to Mishael, Meshach; and to Azariah, Abednego.*"

God's children are called to recognize the value He places on them and to remain steadfast in their faith, avoiding entanglements that compromise their allegiance to Him. When we as God's children join these types of secret society organizations, we inadvertently can cause others to be drawn into them as people look at us as the model to be followed. By understanding these biblical examples, believers can discern the intentions behind invitations to join such covenants and choose to remain faithful to God.

Do Our Words Matter?

Lastly, some may ask the question, do our words matter? Yes, our words matter significantly. The **Bible** underscores the importance of our words and the impact they have on our lives and others. In *Matthew 12:36-37*, **Jesus** emphasizes, "*But I say unto you, That every idle word that men shall speak, they shall give account thereof in the day of judgment. For by thy words thou shalt be justified, and by thy words thou shalt be condemned*." This passage makes it clear that our words are not trivial; they have lasting consequences and we'll be held accountable for them. *Proverbs 18:21* further reinforces this idea: "*Death and life are in the power of the tongue: And they that love it shall eat the fruit thereof*." Our words can bring about life or death, highlighting their profound power and significance. Moreover, **Jesus** teaches that it's not what goes into a person's mouth that defiles them, but what comes out, as stated in *Matthew 15:11*: "*Not that which goeth into the mouth defileth a man; but that which cometh out of the mouth, this defileth a man*." This reinforces the idea that our words reflect our inner character and can either purify or corrupt us. *Numbers 30:2* also reminds us of the gravity of our vows and promises: "*If a man vow a vow unto the LORD, or swear* *an oath to bind his soul with a bond; he shall not break his word, he shall do according to all that proceedeth out of his mouth*." Our words and promises bind us, and we must honor them.

Is Ignorance of God's Law An Excuse?

The Bible warns us that ignorance can lead to destruction. *Hosea 4:6* states, "*My people are destroyed for lack of knowledge: because thou hast rejected knowledge, I will also reject thee, that thou shalt be no priest to me: seeing thou hast forgotten the law of thy God, I will also forget thy children*." This verse highlights the peril of ignorance, particularly ignorance of God's laws and principles. It underscores the necessity of seeking knowledge and understanding to avoid the dire consequences of ignorance. In both a spiritual and legal context, ignorance of the law is not considered a valid excuse. This fundamental legal principle is upheld in the U.S. legal system, asserting that ignorance of the law is no defense. If ignorance were accepted as an excuse, any person charged with a criminal offense could claim ignorance to avoid the consequences. Laws apply to every person within the jurisdiction, whether they're known or understood. Similarly, in a spiritual sense, God's laws and commandments apply to everyone, and we're expected to seek and adhere to **His** knowledge. The consequences of not knowing God's laws can be severe, reinforcing the need to continually seek His wisdom and guidance.

Conclusion

Altars, rituals, oaths, and covenants are integral components of many secret societies. While these elements aren't inherently evil of themselves, their use in ways that contradict God's commands and principles isn't good. The **Bible** provides clear guidance on how these practices should be conducted in a manner that honors God. As Christians, it's crucial to discern and avoid involvement in practices that lead away from the truth of scripture and the exclusive worship of the one true **God**. By understanding the biblical perspective on these elements, believers can better navigate the spiritual landscape and remain faithful to their calling in **Christ**.

9

"There is nothing from without a man, that entering into him can defile him: but the things which come out of him, those are they that defile the man." (Mark 7:15 KJV)

In this chapter, we confront the sobering reality of the consequences of participation in secret societies. Through a discerning examination of both the tangible and spiritual repercussions, we'll uncover the detrimental effects that membership in these organizations can have on individuals, families, and communities.

Spiritual Bondage

•**Entanglement In Darkness**: Participation in secret societies often leads to spiritual bondage, as individuals become ensnared in the web of secrecy and deception. *Ephesians 6:12 ("For our struggle is not against flesh and blood, but against the rulers, against the authorities, against the powers of this dark world and against the spiritual forces of evil in the heavenly realms")* reminds us of the spiritual battle at hand.

•**Oppression & Manipulation**: Secret societies wield a powerful influence over their members, employing tactics of manipulation and control to maintain their grip. This spiritual oppression can manifest in various forms, including emotional turmoil, relational strife, and a deepening sense of spiritual emptiness.

Moral Compromise

•**Erosion of Ethics**: Participation in secret societies often necessitates a compromise of ethical principles and moral values. *Proverbs 11:3* (*"The integrity of the upright guides them, but the unfaithful are destroyed by their duplicity"*) warns of the destructive consequences of moral compromise.

•**Sacrificing Convictions**: Members may find themselves pressured to engage in unethical or immoral behavior to maintain their standing within the organization. This erosion of integrity can have far-reaching consequences, tarnishing reputations and undermining personal character.

Familial & Social Impact

•**Estrangement and Isolation**: Participation in secret societies can lead to estrangement from family members and loved ones who don't share the same beliefs or values. **Luke 12:53** (*"They will be divided, father against son and son against father, mother against daughter and daughter against mother"*) highlights the potential for division within families.

•**Social Stigma**: Individuals associated with secret societies may face social stigma and ostracization from their communities. This isolation can further deepen the sense of alienation and loneliness experienced by members, exacerbating the negative impact on their mental and emotional well-being.

Spiritual Consequences

●**Separation From God**: Ultimately, participation in secret societies can lead to a spiritual separation from God. *Isaiah 59:2* ("*But your iniquities have separated you from your God; your sins have hidden his face from you, so that he will not hear*") underscores the spiritual consequences of willful disobedience and rebellion.

●**Loss of Spiritual Fulfillment**: As individuals become increasingly entangled in the web of secrecy and deception, they may experience a profound sense of spiritual emptiness and dissatisfaction. This loss of spiritual fulfillment can have lasting implications for their overall well-being and sense of purpose.

Personal Testimony

In my journey, I experienced firsthand the spiritual bondage and moral compromise that accompanied membership in a secret society. The pressure to conform to unethical practices and the strain it placed on my relationships with loved ones left me feeling isolated and spiritually adrift. It wasn't until I turned away from the allure of secrecy and deception, and embraced the light of God's truth, that I found true freedom and fulfillment in His presence. My testimony serves as a reminder of the profound impact that participation in secret societies can have on one's life, and the transformative power of God's grace to bring healing and restoration. I'll expound more about my testimony in the next chapter.

In conclusion, the consequences of participation in secret societies are far-reaching and profound. From spiritual bondage and moral compromise to familial estrangement and social stigma, the detrimental effects of membership in these organizations cannot be overstated. As believers, we must heed the warnings of scripture and guard against the allure of secrecy and deception. By remaining steadfast in our faith and devotion to **God**, we can avoid the pitfalls of spiritual compromise and experience true freedom and fulfillment in His presence.

Just because it's part of our culture, doesn't mean God is pleased with it. (Colossians 2:8)

#BeNotDeceived

Quote by Tommy Arbuckle

10

Chapter 10 From Bonds to Liberation: A Testimony of Renouncing Secret Societies

"And they overcame him by the blood of the Lamb, and by the word of their testimony; and they loved not their lives unto the death." (**Revelation 12: 11 KJV**)

In 1994, I embarked on a significant journey by joining *Prince Hall Freemasonry*, drawn by the understanding and assurances that it was a **Christian** organization. Like many others, I was influenced by the fact that many of its members were professing believers, framing it as a path aligned with my faith values. A year later, in the Spring of 1995, this journey into fraternity life deepened when I was initiated into *Omega Psi Phi Fraternity, Inc.* at **Prairie View A&M University**, a **Historically Black College & University** (**HBCU**). Both affiliations promised a sense of belonging and a robust support network, steeped in traditions that resonated within the *Black* community and echoed my family legacy. Yet, amidst these bonds of brotherhood and the allure of shared heritage, I faced a transformative challenge. In April 1997, I received my calling to be a **Minister**, which unveiled a profound conflict between the commitments I made to these organizations and the mandates of my **Christian** faith. This calling compelled me to confront the rituals and oaths I embraced in both *Freemasonry* and *Omega Psi Phi* and to measure them against the truth of what God said in His word. This confrontation would challenge the very foundations of my identity and allegiance, setting me on a path of profound spiritual introspection and transformation.

1.   Early Days in *Prince Hall Freemasonry* and *Omega Psi Phi*

Joining *Prince Hall Freemasonry*

In 1994, motivated by a search for deeper community and spiritual alignment, I joined *Prince Hall Freemasonry*. My decision was heavily influenced by the organization's reputation as a *Christian* fraternity, where many members were also professing believers. My mother was a member of the *Eastern Star* and when I asked about the organization, she didn't offer any objections to me joining. I knew little to nothing about the organization other than what I was told; that it's a *Christian* fraternity. The appeal was strong; it seemed a place where faith and brotherhood intersected, offering both spiritual enrichment and communal support. I was drawn to the idea of being part of a lineage that not only celebrated **African American** heritage but also held a commitment to *Christian* values, as I understood them.

Joining *Omega Psi Phi Fraternity, Inc*.

The following year, my fraternity journey expanded as I pledged to be a member of *Omega Psi Phi* at the *Rho Theta Chapter* located at *Prairie View A&M University*. This decision was layered with familial influences—my older brother was a member, and his experiences painted a picture of a brotherhood rich in support, excellence, and communal achievement. *Omega Psi Phi* presented itself as more than just a social organization; it was a network of motivated *Black* professionals who strived for societal impact and

95

personal growth. The fraternity's deep roots in educational achievement and leadership within the *Black* community were compelling. It promised a platform for both personal development and a way to contribute meaningfully to the broader *African American* narrative. Both of these affiliations initially seemed to complement my desires for fellowship and spiritual growth, framed by their historical significance and professed values. However, as I would learn through my calling and subsequent spiritual awakening, the true nature of these commitments would test my faith and force me to reconsider what it truly means to walk in alignment with God's word.

2. God's Calling

My spiritual awakening began shortly after I settled into my roles within *Prince Hall Freemasonry* and *Omega Psi Phi*. In April 1997, I received a profound calling to ministry, an event that marked a pivotal turn in my faith journey. **God spoke directly to me**; I didn't know that God talked. I was so entrenched in sin, I was in complete shock that He was talking to me, let alone calling me. This calling was not just a call to preach but a divine invitation to scrutinize and realign my life's commitments with the teachings of *Christ*.

As I went deeper into my ministerial studies and grew in my relationship with **God**, I started to experience a series of revelatory dreams and unmistakable signs that challenged my affiliations with both organizations. **God** asked me a question about *Freemasonry*, He said *"**Are you still with that**? **Because I am not in that**!"* These spiritual experiences brought to light the conflicting aspects of the oaths I took and the rituals I participated in, many of which mirrored each other between the *Masonic* and *Omega* rites. The more I reflected on these experiences, the more I realized the rituals and oaths, which I once believed were benign or even spiritually neutral, held elements that weren't in harmony with biblical teachings. This realization was particularly jarring given the initial belief that my *Masonic* ties were grounded in Christian principles. Scriptures such as **2 Corinthians 6:14**, "***Do not be unequally yoked with unbelievers. For what partnership has righteousness with lawlessness? Or what fellowship has light with darkness***?" became a cornerstone of my spiritual dilemma. These verses prompted a deep and often uncomfortable reevaluation of what it meant to serve **God** wholeheartedly and without compromise. This period of spiritual awakening was challenging, as it stirred a sense of spiritual dissonance that I could no longer ignore. It compelled me to question not just the practices I adopted but also the very foundation of my identity as a *Christian* and community leader. As I continued to pray and seek divine guidance, it became increasingly clear that my path to true spiritual integrity might require difficult choices and significant changes in my life.

3. Pulling Away

As the weight of my spiritual awakening grew, I began to consciously distance myself from actively participating in *Prince Hall Freemasonry* and *Omega Psi Phi* activities. This decision wasn't taken lightly, it involved stepping back from friends who offered significant personal and professional support. Initially, I ceased wearing any paraphernalia associated with these organizations and reduced my attendance at their meetings and social events. This phase of withdrawal was driven by a deep desire to align more closely with my *Christian* convictions, as I sought to be a light within these groups without partaking in activities that conflicted with my faith. I hoped my more subdued and reflective actions might serve as a silent testimony to those still in the fraternity and others who were Masons. My intent wasn't to judge their individual choices but to reconsider my own in the light of the revelations I received. During this time, I wrestled with the possibility that I could influence these organizations positively from within. I pondered if my continued but altered presence could spark a dialogue about faith and integrity, perhaps guiding others toward reevaluating their spiritual and moral alignments. Yet, even as I grappled with these thoughts, I felt a growing unease that mere presence wasn't enough and a more definitive action might be necessary. I decided to completely renounce *Freemasonry* and *Omega Psi Phi* based on what **God** said to me and to stop talking to anyone who I knew was a member of either organization. I didn't have revelation as to why **God** said He wasn't in them but I had information and that was enough for me to renounce both of them. This period of separation and disassociation by pulling away was crucial—it was a time of introspection and prayer, seeking clarity from **God** on how best to proceed. Each step away from my previous commitments brought a mixture of relief and apprehension as I navigated the complex interplay of community ties, personal faith, and the calling I felt to uphold a higher standard of spiritual commitment.

4. Slipping Backwards

As my relationship with God deepened, I occasionally returned to attend the *Panhellenic* events hosted by all of the *BGLOs* known as the *Divine Nine*, such as scholarship balls, and picnics, not as an active member of *Omega Psi Phi* adorned in *Greek* paraphernalia, but as a friend. I believed by attending, I was given a divine opportunity to act as a beacon of light to them. My familiarity with many of them, some being close friends since before our fraternal bonds, fueled this belief. This period also coincided with my wife becoming a member of *Delta Sigma Theta*, which led us to attend various *BGLO* events together. I didn't know much about other *BGLOs* and she said *Delta Sigma Theta* was different than the others because it was based on *Christian* values. She was engaged with the Delta's activities far more than I was with the Omega's, yet her involvement eventually nudged me back towards a fraternity presence from which I stepped away from. Gradually, I found myself being drawn back into wearing *Omega* paraphernalia, albeit lightly. It started with a shirt gifted by my wife, emblazoned with "*Omega's for Christ*," which seemed a harmless nod to my faith within the fraternity context. This blending of my spiritual identity with fraternity affiliation tricked me into a false sense of security. My participation remained light—I avoided chapter meetings and similar gatherings but would attend casual events like picnics or golf outings. At these gatherings, when fraternity songs played, I found myself altering the lyrics, substituting *"Omega"* with "**Jesus**" in songs like *"All of My Love."* This adjustment reflected my inner conflict; it felt wrong to dedicate such words to anything but **Christ**. I convinced myself that these changes were enough to align my fraternity involvement with my faith. *Omega Psi Phi* was, in my view, just a historical *Black* social service organization—an extension of the community and a network of old college friends, not an idol in my heart. Yet, what I didn't realize was how **God** viewed my divided allegiances. Despite my intentions and the modifications I made, my ongoing association with the fraternity was displeasing to Him. Unbeknownst to me, this displeasure was manifesting as a spiritual burden, placing a curse upon myself and my family—a stark reminder of the severe implications of divided loyalties and the subtle ways secular commitments can conflict with divine commands.

5. Revelations and Encounters

Deception Exposed

A defining moment in my journey of spiritual realignment occurred during the spring of 2022. I was at home and began pondering my life. I started to consider all of what I experienced in **God** which far exceeded my expectations of what I thought my life would be. While doing so, I sensed **God** had more for me, so I grabbed my **Bible** and came across the scripture, *Isaiah 5:20* which states *"**Woe unto them that call evil good, and good evil; that put darkness for light, and light for darkness; that put bitter for sweet, and sweet for bitter**!"* Although I read this verse before, this time I had a profound feeling there was deception in my life. I told God I was willing to unlearn things and start from scratch to be taught the truth. So I laid prostrate on the floor and cried out with an earnest prayer saying *"God, if there is anything in my life, that I thought was true but was a lie or anything in my life I thought was a lie but was true or anything in my life that I thought was evil but it was good or anything I thought was good but it was evil, Lord reveal this to me so that I can be pleasing to you and not walk in deception."* After getting off the floor, the **Holy Spirit** took me on a journey through the scriptures teaching me about deception in ways I hadn't previously heard or understood before.

For us to be deceived, it must be by things we consider natural to us, if it's abnormal, we'll automatically reject it. Deception will most likely have 95% truth in it to draw us in, so the 5% lie deceives us. Counterfeit money is a powerful metaphor for understanding the nature and impact of deception. When counterfeit currency slips past banking checkpoints, it can circulate undetected for years, mingling seamlessly with genuine notes. This persistence in circulation underscores how effective and damaging deception can be once it goes unrecognized or overlooked. Like deception, counterfeit money capitalizes on its close resemblance to the real thing. Counterfeiters strive to achieve a 95% accuracy rate in mimicking authentic currency. This high degree of similarity is what makes counterfeit money so deceptive; it looks, feels, and may seem to weigh the same as legitimate currency to the untrained eye. In the same way, deception often presents itself as almost indistinguishable from the truth, using superficial similarities and partial truths to blend in and pass initial scrutiny. This process illustrates the dangerous potential of deception to infiltrate and corrupt systems—whether financial, social, or spiritual—by exploiting familiarity and trust. Just as counterfeit money uses its likeness to real currency to circulate among us, deceptive ideas or doctrines can spread within families, churches, and communities causing confusion and harm before they're recognized and rectified. Understanding the characteristics of genuine currency, whether in banking or knowledge, is crucial to protecting oneself against the pitfalls of sophisticated fakes that aim to deceive and exploit us.

As *Christians*, it's natural for us to want to praise, worship, pray, and serve others. However, just because you and I hear someone pray and use the name of **Jesus** doesn't mean **Jesus** is in agreement and/or authorizing what they're doing. Just because we see a **Bible** on a table and someone lighting candles doesn't mean **God** is pleased with what's happening. When we hear these things or see someone doing these types of things, we automatically think **God** is involved but this isn't always true. In *Luke 4:1-12*, the narrative of **Jesus'** temptation in the wilderness provides a profound exploration of deception and the power of scripture both to defend against and to perpetrate deceit. This passage is critical for understanding how scripture can be employed in spiritual warfare and the subtleties of deception that can occur through the use of holy texts.

Jesus, after fasting for forty days, is physically vulnerable and in this state, He's confronted by Satan, who presents a series of temptations aimed at exploiting **Jesus'** human needs and divine mission. The temptations begin with the devil urging **Jesus** to turn stones into bread, appealing to His physical hunger to undermine His spiritual purpose. **Jesus** counters this temptation with scripture, quoting ***Deuteronomy 8:3*** *"**Man shall not live by bread alone**."* The devil's second attempt involves showing **Jesus** all the kingdoms of the world, promising Him authority over them if He worships Satan. Again, **Jesus** responds with scripture, this time quoting ***Deuteronomy 6:13***: *"**Worship the Lord your God and serve him only**."* However, the third temptation illustrates a cunning twist in the devil's strategy. Satan himself quotes scripture, using ***Psalm 91:11-12*** to suggest that **Jesus** should throw Himself down from the pinnacle of the temple, asserting that **God** would command angels to protect Him. Here, Satan uses scripture not as a means of divine instruction or inspiration but as a tool for deception, twisting its intent to provoke **Jesus** into proving His divinity and **God's** protection spectacularly and unnecessarily. **Jesus'** response to this misuse of scripture is pivotal, He rebuts Satan's deception with another passage from ***Deuteronomy 6:16***: *"**Do not put the Lord your God to the test**."* This response underscores a critical aspect of handling Scripture: the importance of context and intention. **Jesus** demonstrates that knowing scripture isn't merely about recitation but understanding its more profound meaning and application. He shows that the '**Word of God**' must be used with reverence for its context and purpose, not manipulated to serve wrongful ends.

This encounter between **Jesus** and Satan in *Luke 4:1-12* vividly illustrates the dual nature of scripture as both a defensive tool against deception and a potential weapon for deceit when mishandled or manipulated. It highlights the need for discernment and a deep, moral understanding of biblical teachings to ensure they're not used to deceive or justify wrongful actions. This narrative serves as a reminder that even the most sacred texts can be twisted, emphasizing the need for spiritual vigilance and integrity in interpreting and applying **God's word**.

Deception in the biblical context often leverages familiarity to mislead, using names and terms that resonate with believers to introduce subtle yet profound errors. A poignant example of this is seen in the genealogies of Cain and Seth, the sons of Adam, where similar names appear in both lineages, potentially confusing. In the genealogy outlined in *Genesis*, we find that Cain, who was separated from **God** after murdering his brother Abel, named one of his descendants Enoch (*Genesis 4:17*) and Lamech (*Genesis 4:18*). Similarly, Seth, who was born later and considered the appointed child through whom the godly lineage would continue (*Genesis 4:25*), also had a descendant named Enoch (*Genesis 5:6*) and Lamech (*Genesis 5:25*). This repetition of names could easily lead to confusion; although they share names, these individuals represent very different spiritual legacies—one aligned with Cain's rebellion and the other with Seth's godliness.

This principle of using familiar names to deceive is also critically discussed by **Jesus** in *Matthew 24:5*, where He warns His disciples: *"**For many shall come in my name, saying, I am Christ; and shall deceive many**."* Here, **Jesus** points out that false prophets and deceivers will exploit His name—**the name above all names**, familiar and revered among believers—to lead people astray. The familiarity of the name "**Christ**" could be misused to lend credibility to deceptive teachings, misleading those who are not vigilant. The *Apostle Paul* further expands on this concept in *2 Corinthians 11:4*, warning the *Corinthian* church about those who preach "**another Jesus**" or bring "**another spirit**" or "**another gospel**." Paul emphasizes that even if these figures use the name "**Jesus**," the content of their teachings can be fundamentally different and deceptive. The use of the name "**Jesus**" in their preaching doesn't authenticate their message if their teachings contradict the apostolic doctrine and the nature of **Christ** as revealed in scripture. Paul's caution shows that hearing a familiar and sacred name like **Jesus** doesn't guarantee the authenticity of the teaching associated with it. Believers must discern whether the **Jesus** being preached is the **Jesus** of the **Bible—whose gospel is based on grace, truth, and the transformation of lives**—or a distorted version intended to deceive and lead into error. These scriptural examples underscore the need for discernment in the Christian Walk. Deception often wears a mask of familiarity, using names and terms that are dear and sacred to believers to introduce teachings that are contrary to the **word of God**. It highlights the importance of being deeply rooted in scripture and led by the **Holy Spirit** to distinguish between truth and error, ensuring that our faith remains anchored in the true teachings of **Christ** and not swayed by every wind of doctrine.

Deception can play a critical role in our lives, often leading to irreversible consequences, even for the biblical patriarchs and key figures of faith. **Jesus**, fully aware of the challenges that would continue to plague humanity after His ascension, emphasized the importance of vigilance against deception. In *Matthew 24:1-5, 21-25*, Jesus explicitly warns His disciples about the pervasive risk of being misled. He cautions that false prophets will come in His name, claiming, "*I am the Christ*," and will deceive many. Even more dire, **Jesus** predicts the deception in the last days will be so severe that "*if it were possible, they shall deceive the very elect*." This warning highlights the critical need for discernment, especially as believers navigate a world rife with spiritual and moral pitfalls. This theme of the severe consequences of deception is reiterated by Paul in *Galatians 6:7*, "*Be not deceived; God is not mocked: for whatsoever a man soweth, that shall he also reap*." This verse underscores a universal principle: our actions have consequences, and no amount of deception can shield us from the repercussions of our choices. This principle ties back to the *Genesis* account of Eve in the *Garden of Eden*. Despite being deceived by the serpent (*Genesis 3*), Eve—and Adam, who followed her lead—faced severe consequences for their disobedience. Although Eve was beguiled, **God** held her accountable for her actions, leading to the curse that affected not just her but all of humanity. This narrative establishes an essential biblical truth: being deceived doesn't absolve one from the consequences of one's actions.

Another profound example of the irreversible impact of deception is found in the story of Isaac and his sons, Jacob and Esau, in **Genesis 27**. Isaac, intending to bless his firstborn, Esau, was deceived by Jacob and his mother Rebekah. Jacob, disguised as Esau, received the blessings intended for his brother. When the deceit was uncovered, Isaac, despite being deceived and recognizing the switch, couldn't retract the blessing he gave to Jacob. This narrative not only highlights the potency of deception but also the binding nature of words and promises once given, even under false pretenses. Similarly, a stark illustration of the consequences of deception is found in the story of the Gibeonites in **Joshua 9:1-27**. Here, the Gibeonites, fearing the Israelites, resorted to deceit by disguising themselves as weary travelers from a distant land. They convinced the Israelites to enter into a covenant with them, claiming they weren't local inhabitants whom the Israelites were commanded to drive out. The Israelites, failing to seek divine guidance, swore an oath to them. When the deception was revealed, the covenant couldn't be broken because it was sworn by the name of the **Lord**. This event highlights a critical failure: the Israelites didn't "ask counsel at the mouth of the **LORD**," leading them to make a grievous error with long-term consequences. These scriptural accounts are a powerful reminder that deception can entrap even the chosen and the faithful if they're not vigilant. They emphasize the importance of seeking God's guidance in every decision and remaining grounded in His word. For believers today, these lessons are vital. In an era where truth can often be obscured, and falsehoods abound, the necessity of divine wisdom and the commitment to live by God's statutes are more crucial than ever. The call to vigilance is clear—deception is a potent tool against which only spiritual discernment, grounded in prayer and scripture, can effectively guard.

The Omega Scholarship Picnic

The next expansion of God's revelation to me happened during the summer of 2022 at an *Omega Psi Phi Scholarship Picnic*, an event meant to celebrate academic achievements and support young scholars. The event was set against a backdrop of festivity and camaraderie, ostensibly embodying the fraternity's values of uplift and community support. One of my daughters was among the recipients, which added a personal layer of pride to the occasion. However, as the event unfolded, my sense of unease grew. During the step show performed by the newest fraternity members, known as neophytes, the atmosphere took on a different tone. The language and actions during their performance were not only inappropriate but starkly contrasted with the values I strove to uphold in my Christian Walk. Their words, not suitable for the mixed audience of families gathered, hinted at a disconnect between the fraternity's public persona and the behaviors it cultivated behind closed doors. As the performance concluded and the familiar strains of *George Clinton's "Atomic Dog"* filled the air—a song traditionally associated with *Omega Psi Phi* stepping— it wasn't just the revelry that struck me but a palpable spiritual discord. Watching from the sidelines, I saw more than just fraternity brothers stepping in unison; I perceived in the spirit the presence of a demon on every member of the organization throughout the crowd. It was as though with each step and chant, a deeper bond than mere brotherhood was being celebrated—one with an evil presence that troubled my spirit. This visual and spiritual discordance brought a profound discomfort that I couldn't ignore. It was a stark illustration of the divide between the environment I was in and where I felt called to be. The joyous occasion masked an undercurrent of behaviors and associations that now appeared misaligned with the values of the faith I professed. It was a pivotal moment that crystallized my concerns about my continued affiliation with *Omega Psi Phi*. Driven by these revelations, I left the picnic with a heavy heart, the joy of my daughter's achievement overshadowed by a deeper call to action. This experience catalyzed my resolve to seek further clarity and guidance on how to reconcile my role as a father, a minister, and a member of an organization that was increasingly at odds with my spiritual convictions. As I returned home, the need for decisive action was clear, setting the stage for the significant changes that would soon follow in my life.

6. A Divine Directive

The discomfort from the *Omega Scholarship Picnic* was a significant turning point, but it was what happened afterward that truly shook my foundations. After returning home from the picnic, I quickly went and got into my prayer posture to inquire of God. I asked God for clarity and direction, seeking to understand what I saw and the unease in my spirit. In response, I heard **God** tell me to read Derek Prince's book, "***Blessings or Curse***: ***You Can Choose***," which had been untouched on my bookshelf for over twenty years. This wasn't just a random choice; God directed me to it as a source of answers.

As I read the book, God spoke to me through its pages, making it clear that the oaths and commitments I made to these organizations were not as harmless as I once believed. Eventually, I came across a chapter in the book about false gods explaining how Freemasonry, Fraternities, and Sororities were considered idolatrous in the eyes of God. *Exodus 20:3-5* forms a central part of the *Ten Commandments*, delivering a clear directive against idolatry. It states, "*You shall have no other gods before me. You shall not make for yourself a carved image, or any likeness of anything that is in heaven above, or that is on the earth beneath, or that is in the water under the earth. You shall not bow down to them or serve them, for I the Lord your God am a jealous God, visiting the iniquity of the fathers on the children to the third and the fourth generation of those who hate me*." This passage underscores the severity with which God views the act of idolatry. Not only is it considered a betrayal of the covenant relationship between God and His people, but it also invokes a curse that can extend to affect a person and their future generations. This reflects the profound spiritual and communal consequences of idolatry, indicating that such actions disrupt the foundational order and harmony intended by God. In *Matthew 6:24*, Jesus articulates a related principle that deepens our understanding of idolatry: "*No one can serve two masters. Either you will hate the one and love the other, or you will be devoted to the one and despise the other*." While this verse is often interpreted in the context of the relationship between God and material wealth ("*You cannot serve both God and money*."), it also pertains broadly to the divided loyalties that idolatry represents. Idolatry, at its core, is an allegiance to something other than God, which inevitably leads to a divided heart and spiritual disloyalty. This division is something **God** doesn't take lightly, as it fundamentally undermines the exclusive devotion that's due to Him alone. The connection between *Exodus 20:3-5* and *Matthew 6:24* highlights a consistent biblical theme: God demands and deserves undivided spiritual allegiance. Any deviation from this—whether through the worship of other gods, the creation of idols, or the prioritization of worldly wealth—constitutes a serious violation of the relationship we're called to have with Him. The consequences of such actions, as noted in *Exodus*, aren't only personal but can have ramifications that affect one's family for generations, emphasizing the lasting impact of our spiritual choices. This intergenerational aspect of the curse serves as a sobering reminder of the long-term effects of our actions and the responsibility we have to uphold our devotion to God without compromise.

My act of idolatry, whether it was intentional or unintentional violated the commandment of God with its due penalty. When I joined each of the secret societies, I was between 20-21 years old and severely spiritually immature. As the **Holy Spirit** continued to enlighten me, He showed me how each of the organizations had its own ritual, ritual book, altar, prayer, hymn, and memorial service for deceased members. Some of the Greek-lettered fraternities and sororities organizations have false Greek gods in their ritual book which states they look to these false Greek

111

gods for spiritual assistance. I quickly realized they're not traits of just a social service organization but a false religion. We had to bow down to the altar of these organizations and swear an oath that also violated God's word (**Matthew 5:34**). **God** revealed to me that my continued association with secret societies was in direct conflict with the life He intended for me. This revelation was specific and pointed—I wasn't merely interpreting feelings or signs; **God** was telling me explicitly through the pages of the book and the **Bible** that I needed to sever these ties if I was to walk in obedience to Him. The spiritual ties and pledges of allegiance I took were creating barriers between me and God's plans for my life. It was a direct revelation from **God** that these bonds had placed me, and my family, under a curse—a stark and troubling realization. So, what is a curse you may ask? How can a **man of God**, be under a curse? I'll discuss aspects of a curse in more detail in the next section. This divine directive wasn't easy to digest. It demanded significant changes, not just spiritually but socially and personally, as these organizations were intertwined with many aspects of my life. But the message from God was clear and non-negotiable: I needed to renounce my memberships and realign my commitments solely with God's word. Armed with this directive from God, I prepared myself for the difficult conversations and actions ahead. It was daunting, but the need for spiritual integrity and obedience to God's command outweighed any human ties or past commitments. This was about ensuring my walk with God was pure and undivided, recognizing true freedom and spiritual health in my life depended on my response to His call.

7. Understanding The Nature of A Curse

As Christians, we are called to a life of obedience and righteousness, and we must never take the grace bestowed upon us through **Christ** for granted. In *Romans 6:15*, Paul poses a critical question: "*What then? Shall we sin because we are not under the law but under grace*? **By no means**!" This challenges the notion that grace may be used as a license to continue in sin. Instead, grace empowers us to break free from the bondage of sin and align our lives with God's commandments.

Paul elaborates on the severe consequences of sin in *Romans 6:23*, "*For the wages of sin is death, but the gift of God is eternal life in Christ Jesus our Lord*." This stark contrast underscores that, despite the redemption available through **Jesus**, the inherent consequences of sin—spiritual death and separation from God—persist as active forces in the world. These consequences remind us that our actions have profound spiritual implications, even under the covenant of grace. This principle is vividly illustrated in *Acts 5:1-10*, the story of Ananias and Sapphira. Despite being believers in the early *Christian* community—a community marked by mutual support and grace—when Ananias and Sapphira lied about the proceeds from a sale of property, they both fell dead. This severe outcome occurred after the death, burial, and resurrection of **Jesus Christ**, demonstrating that God's judgment can still manifest in immediate physical consequences for sin, even among believers. Their story serves as a sobering reminder that the *New*

Testament grace doesn't eliminate the temporal consequences of deceit and disobedience.

Numbers 14:18 emphasizes the attributes of God, stating, *"The Lord is slow to anger, abounding in love and forgiving sin and rebellion. Yet He does not leave the guilty unpunished; He punishes the children for the sin of the parents to the third and fourth generation."* This verse highlights God's graciousness and His mercy, yet it also underscores His justice and the consequences of sin. Following this, *Exodus 33:19* further illustrates how God exercises His sovereign choice in dispensing His grace and mercy, declaring, *"I will be gracious to whom I will be gracious, and will show mercy on whom I will show mercy."* This assertion confirms that God alone decides whom to extend His grace and mercy to, a choice beyond human influence or entitlement. These declarations show God's distribution of mercy is not arbitrary but is part of His divine prerogative, a decision that reflects His more profound knowledge of human hearts and situations. Such sovereignty is meant to affirm God's omnipotence and lead us toward repentance, as reinforced by *2 Peter 3:9*, which reminds us that God is patient with us, not wanting anyone to perish but everyone to come to repentance. This patience is an expression of His grace, intended not as an excuse for us to continue in sin but as an opportunity to realign our lives with His will walking in obedience.

Jesus exemplifies and teaches the importance of obedience through suffering. *Hebrews 5:8* tells us, *"Although he was a son, he learned obedience from what he suffered."* This passage reveals that even

Christ, who was without sin, underwent suffering as part of His human experience, which refined His obedience and submission to the Father's will. This principle applies to us as followers of **Christ**; often, it's through the difficulties and trials we face that we learn true obedience and the depth of our reliance on **God** turning away from sin. Furthermore, in *John 5:14*, after healing a man who was invalid for 38 years, **Jesus** offers a stern warning: *"See, you are well again. Stop sinning or something worse may happen to you."* This admonition illustrates that while **Jesus'** sacrifice on the cross offers' forgiveness and reconciliation with **God**, it doesn't nullify the natural consequences of our actions or the spiritual laws that govern the universe. Sin still has the potential to produce adverse outcomes in our lives, and ongoing disobedience can lead to greater spiritual and physical afflictions. **Jesus'** instruction to *"sin no more"* underscores the responsibility that comes with receiving God's grace. We shouldn't abuse this gift but live in a way that reflects our transformation—walking in obedience and righteousness. **Jesus'** death, burial, and resurrection provide the means for salvation and reconciliation, but they also call us to a higher standard of living. As believers seated with **Christ** in heavenly places (*Ephesians 2:6*), we must actively choose to forsake sin and embrace a life that honors **God**. In essence, while the grace of **God** through **Jesus Christ** covers all sin and offers us eternal life, it also requires a response of continual obedience and holiness. We must heed the lessons taught through scripture and by **Christ**, avoiding sin and its destructive impact on our lives. This isn't merely to escape negative consequences but to live fully in the freedom and victory that **Christ** has secured for us. So, what happens when we choose to walk in sin, in disobedience to God's commandments, a curse can be applied to our life. A curse is a form of judgment and punishment that **God** uses as a consequence of disobedience to His commands, impacting both **Christians** and **non-Christians** alike. This concept is rooted deeply in scripture and reflects the serious implications of our actions concerning God's laws.

In the book of *Genesis*, we find a compelling account that illustrates how curses are invoked through disobedience. God explicitly commanded Adam in *Genesis 2:17* not to eat from the tree of the knowledge of good and evil, warning that death would result if he disobeyed. However, Eve and Adam ate the fruit after Eve was deceived by the serpent, leading to severe repercussions for them and the serpent (*Genesis 3:6, 14-17*).

Each curse pronounced by **God** was unique to each of the individual's:

•The serpent was cursed to crawl on its belly all the days of its life.

•Eve was sentenced to great pain in childbirth and the ability to have multiple child conceptions.

•Adam was told because he listened to his wife and ate from the tree, the ground would be cursed because of him, making it difficult to cultivate food.

God is the one who determines what kind of curse is applied to our lives. You and I both could've committed that same sin but have uniquely different curses in our lives. I may not be able to hold a job while you or your spouse can't have children. These curses underscore a profound truth: **God** holds each person accountable for their actions, regardless of the influence or deception we endured by others. Moreover, the scriptures reveal that **God** will allow us to be tempted not as punishment but as a means to prove and test our love and fidelity to Him. *Deuteronomy 13:1-4* warns against following prophets or dreamers who perform signs or wonders yet advocate serving other gods. This passage clarifies that such events are tests from **God**, intended to reveal whether our hearts truly belong to Him. It's a sobering thought that signs and wonders can be instruments of testing, calling us to a deeper discernment and commitment to follow only the **Lord**. It's a stark reminder that being misled by others— whether a spouse, a prophet, or a friend—doesn't absolve us of the consequences of our disobedience.

In *Matthew 23:2-3*, **Jesus** addresses a critical aspect of religious leadership and personal accountability in following scriptural teachings. He tells the crowd and His disciples, "*The teachers of the law and the Pharisees sit in Moses' seat. So you must be careful to do everything they tell you. But do not do what they do, for they do not practice what they preach.*" This directive highlights an essential distinction between the truth of **God's word** and the human imperfections of those who deliver it.

Jesus acknowledges the religious leaders of the time were the authorized interpreters of the *Law of Moses* and, as such, held a position that deserved attention when they accurately conveyed the scriptures. However, He also criticizes these leaders for their hypocrisy and failure to live according to the laws they taught. This hypocrisy undermines their moral and spiritual authority, demonstrating that knowing the law is insufficient without corresponding righteous action. This teaching underscores the perfection of **God's word** as revealed in the scriptures—it's complete, holy, and unerring, serving as the ultimate standard for faith and practice. However, the individuals who teach **God's word** aren't perfect; they're susceptible to the same failings and sins as those they teach, which can lead to contradictions between their words and actions. For followers of **Christ**, this presents a clear directive: We're to model our lives based on the teachings of scripture rather than the actions of human leaders when those actions deviate from Biblical principles. It's crucial to discern and separate the truth of the **word** from the behavior of its proclaimers when they fall short of its standards. This principle is especially relevant in a world where religious leaders hold significant sway over their congregation. Followers must remain vigilant, testing all teachings against the scripture as the Bereans did in *Acts 17:11*, who were commended for verifying Paul's teachings against the scriptures daily. This approach ensures that one's faith practice is built on the solid foundation of **God's word** and not on the potentially flawed interpretations or behaviors of human leaders. While we respect and learn from those in positions of spiritual authority such as Apostles, Pastors, Teachers, Prophets, and

Evangelists, we must critically engage with their teachings, always reverting to scripture as our ultimate guide. In doing so, we maintain the integrity of our faith walk, ensuring it's aligned with the teachings of **Christ** and the apostolic doctrine as intended in the **Holy Scriptures**.

In essence, the dynamics of a curse hinge on our decisions and our response to God's commandments. These biblical examples serve as a cautionary tale, reminding us that our actions have spiritual consequences that can extend beyond our immediate circumstances, affecting our environment and relationships. They emphasize the necessity of aligning our lives with God's commandments and rejecting any influence that might lead us astray.

8. The Lingering Shadows of Deception & Curses

The complexities of deception and the resulting curses are vividly illustrated in the biblical narratives of Joshua and David. Remember in the previous section, how I discussed the Israelites, led by Joshua, who were deceived by the Gibeonites and entered into a covenant with their enemies because they didn't ask counsel of **God**? This decision, though made under deceptive circumstances, bound the Israelites to a covenant that would have lasting implications. Centuries later, the repercussions of this hastily made covenant manifested during the reign of *King David*. The narrative in *2 Samuel 21:1-9* reveals that Israel suffered three years of famine, a devastating curse that perplexed David. It was only when he sought divine insight that the cause of the famine was revealed. **God** disclosed the famine was a punishment for Saul's breach of the covenant with the Gibeonites, where Saul sought to annihilate the Gibeonites in his zeal for Israel and Judah. This disclosure underscores a profound biblical principle: the enduring nature of covenants and the generational impact of curses resulting from their violation. David wasn't King when the acts were committed and had no part in the decision to deceive or breach the covenant with the Gibeonites, found himself dealing with the consequences of actions taken by a previous generation. This situation exemplifies how generational curses can impact descendants, leaving them to face challenges that originated long before their time. The response by David is particularly instructive. Upon learning the cause of the famine, he didn't simply resign to fate; instead, he took proactive steps to rectify the breach of covenant as prescribed by **God**. He met with the Gibeonites, sought their terms for reconciliation, and acted upon them to lift the curse from the people of Israel. This act of seeking and following through on divine guidance not only resolved the immediate crisis but also restored the spiritual and physical health of the nation. This narrative highlights the critical importance of inquiring of **God** in the face of adversities that seem contrary to His promises of blessing. Just as David discovered, sometimes the challenges we face are the repercussions of unaddressed or unknown actions from our past, possibly even from previous generations. It emphasizes, like David, we must actively seek God's face and wisdom when encountering prolonged difficulties or curses, to uncover any hidden breaches or unresolved issues that may be influencing our present. By doing so, we can identify the roots of our troubles and address them according to God's guidance, potentially breaking cycles of suffering and releasing ourselves and future generations from the burdens of inherited curses. This proactive approach not only aligns us more closely with God's will but also enables us to live lives free from the shadows of the past, fully **embraced in the blessings God intends for us.**

9. Called By God Yet Under A Curse

It might seem contradictory for a man of God, especially one endowed with spiritual gifts and a calling, to be under a curse. However, spiritual status or the presence of divine gifts doesn't exempt anyone from the consequences of disobedience or misalignment with God's commands.

Throughout my years of ministry, filled with prophetic insights, healings, and spiritual battles, it became clear these gifts didn't shield me from the repercussions of personal or ancestral disobedience. God's gifts are given freely, as stated in **Romans 11:29**, "**for God's gifts and his call are irrevocable**." This means, that while the gifts themselves are without repentance, our actions can still open doors to spiritual consequences. Scripture provides profound insights into the nature of curses and divine discipline. In the book of **Hebrews**, the relationship between God's love and His discipline is explained: "**And have you forgotten the exhortation that addresses you as sons? My son, do not regard lightly the discipline of the Lord, nor be weary when reproved by him. For the Lord disciplines the one he** *loves, and chastises every son whom he receives*" (*Hebrews 12:5-6*). This passage reveals that discipline, which can include curses or other forms of correction, is a part of God's loving engagement with His children, intended to guide us back to the right path.

The mechanism of a curse as a consequence of disobedience is also clearly articulated in scripture, for instance, in the story of *King Saul*, Israel's first King. Saul was anointed by **God** and started his reign with divine favor. However, his disobedience and failure to follow God's commands led to his downfall. In *1 Samuel 15*, Saul was instructed by God through the prophet Samuel to destroy the Amalekites and all they possessed. Instead, Saul spared the King of Amalek and kept the best of the livestock, directly disobeying God's command. When confronted by Samuel, Saul initially denied his disobedience and later claimed he spared the best of the animals to sacrifice to the **Lord**. Samuel rebuked Saul with the famous words, "*To obey is better than sacrifice, and to heed is better than the fat of rams*" (*1 Samuel 15:22*). Because of his disobedience, **God** cursed Saul's reign, ultimately rejecting him as King and seeking a new leader for Israel who had a heart more aligned with His own. A curse in your life can cause you to lose everything. This story underscores the critical nature of obedience in maintaining God's blessing and the severe consequences of deviating from His explicit instructions. *Deuteronomy 11:26-28* outlines this, emphasizing that blessings come from obedience and curses from disobedience. Moreover, the interplay of generational blessings and curses shows our actions have broader implications beyond our immediate spiritual experiences. In my life, despite having a vibrant ministry, I had to confront the reality that certain afflictions and struggles within my family were the results of unaddressed or unresolved spiritual issues, possibly extending back generations. The concept that a man of **God** can be under a curse, therefore, underscores the need for continual self-examination, repentance, and alignment with God's statutes. Understanding that a curse can affect anyone regardless of their spiritual gifts or ministry achievements brings a sobering clarity to the biblical call to live a life of obedience and holiness, constantly aligned with God's will and His commandments.

10. Confrontation With Truth

After dedicating four months of prayer and studying "*Blessings and Curses*" by *Derek Prince*, a profound understanding began to reshape my perspective on spiritual commitments.

One following Sunday, I was asked to deliver a sermon at my home church. As I prepared my message, I felt a strong prompting from **God**, revealing He spoke to someone in the congregation specifically about me and they hadn't yet shared with me what he said. During the sermon, I addressed the congregation directly about the urgency of aligning our lives with God's truth, emphasizing our actions and decisions could significantly impact not only our spiritual health but also those around us. Inspired by the **Holy Spirit**, I took a moment to share openly that I knew God communicated something about me to someone present. I urged whoever it was to come forward and share their message, stressing the importance of obedience and transparency in our community of faith. This call to action was a crucial moment, not just in my sermon, but in my spiritual journey. I expressed to the congregation that we must be willing to act on the truths **God** reveals to us, even when it requires stepping out in faith and perhaps facing uncomfortable truths. Right after the service, a divine encounter cemented my decision to leave all secret societies. A member of my congregation approached me—hesitant yet compelled by what she felt was a message from **God**. She confirmed precisely what **God** revealed to me: my involvement with the fraternity wasn't pleasing to Him. She told me, "***It's about your fraternity, God is not pleased with it and you being a part of it.***" This external affirmation of my internal struggle was God's way of showing me that my time of decision had arrived. Next, she asked me about my wife and her involvement with her sorority. I knew I had to talk with her and lead my family out of idolatry. Her words were a direct call to action. It wasn't just a personal conviction or an uncomfortable feeling anymore; it was a clear directive from **God**, confirmed through a fellow believer. This confrontation with truth was the final push I needed to make a definitive move. It wasn't enough to quietly step back or modify my involvement; I had to completely sever my ties.

11. Renunciation Actions

Empowered by this clear message from **God**, I took immediate and concrete steps to renounce my memberships. I gathered all items that symbolized my connections to the organizations—paraphernalia, membership certificates, photographs, awards, documents, memorabilia—and burned them. Each item was a reminder of the commitments I once made, and each needed to be addressed as part of my recommitment to **God**. As I stood there watching them burn, I lifted my hands and repented before **God**, renouncing every ungodly oath I took. In response to my actions, I heard the **Lord** say, "*I will have no other gods before me, I will have no other gods before me, I will have no other gods before me.*" I destroyed those items, not out of disrespect for the people I knew in the organization, but as a symbolic act of obedience to God's directive. My heart grieved for the people I knew in the organization, even those I influenced to join as well as for my friends and family members who were still in other secret societies. This physical act of renouncement was a public affirmation of my willingness to obey **God**, marking a new chapter of integrity and faithfulness in my walk with **Christ**. This decision wasn't made lightly, nor was it received without consequence. It required me to forsake deep-seated relationships and step into a place of vulnerability and criticism. Yet, the peace that came with the obedience to renounce the organization was profound. It confirmed that living in truth and alignment with God's will is the foundation of a life truly led by the **Spirit**.

12. Embracing Repentance

True repentance is a pivotal theme throughout scripture, and its significance cannot be overstated, especially in the context of deception and the resulting curses. Repentance is not merely a one-time act of sorrow or regret for wrongs done; it's a transformative process that involves a complete turn-around from sin and a steadfast commitment to walk in obedience to God's commands. The biblical call to repentance is about realignment with God's will, necessitating a profound inner change that manifests in our actions and decisions. It requires acknowledging our missteps and misdeeds, comprehending their impact, and making deliberate efforts to correct our course. This isn't about seeking forgiveness; it's about demonstrating through our behavior that we have indeed turned away from paths of disobedience. In cases where deception leads to unintentional sin or the inheriting of curses, as seen with the Israelites and the covenant with the Gibeonites, repentance plays a crucial role in remediation. It involves recognizing the roots of the issue, often hidden in past actions—either personal or ancestral—and seeking God's guidance for resolution. The act of repentance opens the door for God's mercy and healing, allowing for the restoration of blessings and the lifting of curses.

David's response to the famine caused by Saul's violation of the covenant with the Gibeonites exemplifies active repentance. Upon understanding the spiritual cause of the famine, David didn't merely pray for forgiveness; he sought justice and restoration following God's direction. He engaged the Gibeonites, listened to their grievances, and acted to correct the injustice, thereby upholding the sanctity of the covenant and demonstrating a commitment to righteousness over expediency. Similarly, our approach to repentance should be comprehensive. When we discern our struggles might be linked to spiritual breaches—whether through our actions or as a legacy of past generations—our response should be to seek **God** earnestly. Inquiring of **God**, as David did, leads us to understand not just the nature of our transgression but the steps required to mend our ways.

Moreover, embracing repentance involves embracing God's truth as our moral compass. It compels us to examine our lives critically and continuously, ensuring our daily walk reflects our covenant with **God**. It challenges us to uphold integrity, practice honesty, and embody the values taught by **Christ** in every aspect of our lives. In essence, embracing repentance is about nurturing a heart that's receptive to God's correction and eager to align with His divine statutes. It's about cultivating a lifestyle where our choices and actions consistently reflect our dedication to living out God's will, thereby ensuring our spiritual legacy is one of blessing rather than a curse.

13. Cleansing My House: Family and Broader Impact

After renouncing my affiliation with *Omega Psi Phi*, I recognized a lingering vulnerability within our family due to my wife's active involvement in *Delta Sigma Theta*. Despite her deep commitment to the sorority, which she joined after three attempts, I knew as long as she remained connected, an open door for curses remained over our family. I shared with her everything **God** revealed to me about the curses associated with our involvement in secret societies. It was imperative for her to see the idolatrous nature embedded within *Delta Sigma Theta*. This endeavor was daunting and required a strategic and patient approach, as I anticipated it would be a significant spiritual battle. Over several months, I engaged in fasting and prayer for her deliverance, recognizing she was bound by the ungodly oath she took, which formed a covenant similar to marriage with the organization. To aid in this process, **God** guided me to find *YouTube* videos of testimonials from women who left *Delta Sigma Theta*, highlighting its idolatrous practices. Initially, my wife was resistant and defensive when discussions about her sorority arose. She didn't want to engage and often deflected. However, I persisted, urging her to examine *Delta Sigma Theta's* ritual book with me. **God** equipped me with precise questions and the right timing to have the conversation to guide our review. My first approach was to bring awareness using a subtle approach. I asked her to identify a false god, leading to a discussion on the inappropriateness of having idols in a *Christian* home. I pointed out the sorority's crest, which prominently features the *Greek* goddess Minerva, present on many items in our home. When a person is confronted with the truth, the carnal mind will do everything it can to try and dismiss it. Looking for a way to stay connected with what they want truth to be, even when it's in direct conflict with the word of **God**. *"A carnal mind is enmity against God and it is not subject to the law of God"* (**Romans 8:7**). Next, I showed her how their ritual book stated their members should look to the Greek goddess Minerva for wisdom which contradicted the scriptural command in **James 1:5**, which directs us to seek wisdom from God alone, not from idols or mythological figures. A critical moment occurred when I challenged her understanding of the sorority's rituals. **God** told me to ask her, *"To whom was the altar that you bowed down to erected for*?" Initially, she insisted there was no altar, just a table. After showing her the definition of an altar—a table used for religious purposes—I reiterated my question. This led her to acknowledge that the altar wasn't erected for the **God of the Bible** but for *Delta Sigma Theta*. I then directed her attention to the organization's hymn, which begins with *"Delta*! *With glowing hearts, we praise thee,"* highlighting that such praise should be directed to **God** alone, not to an organization. As months passed, I witnessed a gradual transformation in my wife's perspective. She began to remove *Delta Sigma Theta* paraphernalia and symbols from our home. Her actions weren't all instantaneous, however, I praised **God** for the steps she was making. **God** gave me this principle; **even small steps forward are still considered progress**. One by one, she discarded all of the elephants in our house, statues and paintings. Eventually, she renounced her ties to the sorority, and I led her through a prayer of repentance, breaking every curse associated with it.

However, **God** wasn't finished cleansing our house. One morning, He woke me in the early hours with the words *"Jack and Jill*." At first, I was perplexed, but upon further investigation, I discovered ritualistic elements similar to those in secret societies within *Jack & Jill of America* organization, which our family was also a part of. The organization has its own ritual book, altar, prayer, hymn, and memorial service for deceased members. I was utterly shocked, as I had no idea this was happening within this organization and my wife and children had been subjected to this. This revelation led to a family meeting where I explained the spiritual dangers associated with such practices. I apologized to everyone for my failure as the spiritual leader of our home through deception. We collectively renounced our affiliation with *Jack & Jill of America*, seeking forgiveness for our unintended involvement as a family.

These experiences deeply grieved me as a father and a husband. I realized the gravity of inadvertently leading my family into harmful spiritual territories. ***Ecclesiastes 1:18*** resonated deeply with me during this time, reminding me that ***"in much wisdom is much grief and he that increaseth knowledge increaseth sorrow."*** Meditating on this scripture was such a profound moment as it described the feeling in my heart to help others come into this revelation. God reminded me when he saved me, I had the same feeling and there would be people who would hear me and others who wouldn't. Despite facing ridicule and opposition, I have committed to sharing our family testimony widely, hoping to enlighten others about the hidden spiritual dangers of such affiliations and to encourage other families to seek freedom and cleansing through **Christ**.

God is not pleased with the mixture. Stand for God alone, flee idolatry, witchcraft, and secret sins. (Revelation 3:15-16)

#BeNotDeceived

Quote by Tommy Arbuckle

11

"Because it is written, Be ye holy; for I am holy." (*1 Peter 1:16 KJV*)

In this final chapter, we'll delve into the divine call to **holiness** as outlined in scripture. We'll explore how embracing this call serves as a powerful antidote to the allure of secret societies, offering believers a path of true fulfillment and spiritual abundance.

The Divine Mandate

•**Scriptural Foundation**: The **Bible** echoes the imperative of holiness, emphasizing the sanctity of God's people and their distinctiveness from worldly standards. *Leviticus 20:26* ("*You are to be holy to me because I, the Lord, am holy, and I have set you apart from the nations to be my own*") underscores the divine decree for believers to lead lives consecrated to God's purposes. However, biblical narratives also vividly illustrate instances where individuals failed to uphold this mandate. For instance, King David's adultery with Bathsheba (*2 Samuel 11*) and Solomon's descent into idolatry (*1 Kings 11*) serve as poignant reminders of the consequences of straying from the path of holiness despite their initial devotion to **God**.

•**A Counter-Cultural Lifestyle**: Embracing holiness often requires a radical departure from the values and practices of the surrounding culture. *Romans 12:2* ("*Do not conform to the pattern of this world, but be transformed by the renewing of your mind. Then you will be able to test and approve what God's will is—his* *good, pleasing and perfect will*") challenges believers to resist the pressures of worldly conformity and instead pursue the path of righteousness.

The Pursuit of Purity

●**A Call To Moral Excellence**: Holiness encompasses not only outward behavior but also the inner disposition of the heart. *1 Peter 1:15-16* ("*But just as he who called you is holy, so be holy in all you do; for it is written: 'Be holy, because I am holy*'") encourages believers to strive for moral excellence in every aspect of their lives.

●**Freedom From Moral Compromise**: Embracing holiness liberates believers from the bondage of sin and moral compromise. *2 Corinthians 7:1* ("*Therefore, since we have these promises, dear friends, let us purify ourselves from everything that contaminates body and spirit, perfecting holiness out of reverence for God*") encourages believers to cleanse themselves from all defilement, pursuing holiness out of reverence for **God**.

Cultivating A Life of Integrity

●**Walking In Truth**: Holiness is synonymous with integrity, honesty, and transparency in all dealings. *Psalm 15:1-2* ("*Lord, who may dwell in your sacred tent? Who may live on your holy mountain? The one whose walk is blameless, who does what is righteous, who speaks the truth from their heart*") extols the virtues of those who walk in integrity before **God**.

•**Rejecting the Spirit of Secrecy**: The pursuit of holiness stands in direct opposition to the spirit of secrecy and deception perpetuated by secret societies. *Ephesians 5:8-11* ("*For you were once darkness, but now you are light in the Lord. Live as children of light... Have nothing to do with the fruitless deeds of darkness, but rather expose them*") calls believers to expose the works of darkness and live as children of the light.

Embracing God's Grace

•**Empowered by the Spirit**: The pursuit of holiness is not a solitary endeavor but a partnership with the **Holy Spirit**, who empowers believers to live lives pleasing to God. *Galatians 5:16* ("*So I say, walk by the Spirit, and you will not gratify the desires of the flesh*") reminds believers of the transformative power of the **Spirit** in their lives.

•**Resting in God's Provision**: Holiness is not achieved through human effort alone but through reliance on God's grace and provision. *Philippians 2:13* ("*for it is God who works in you to will and to act in order to fulfill his good purpose*") assures believers that **God** is at work within them, enabling them to live lives that honor and glorify Him.

In conclusion, embracing God's call to holiness offers believers a transformative pathway away from the enticements of secret societies and toward a life of true fulfillment and spiritual abundance. By pursuing moral excellence, cultivating lives of integrity, and relying on the empowering grace of the **Holy Spirit**, believers can walk in the sacredness and separation to which they are called. May this chapter serve as a clarion call to all who seek to honor **God** with their lives, embracing the divine mandate for holiness in every aspect of their being.

Additional Resources

SECRET SOCIETY RENUNCIATION PRAYER

NOTE: This is a guide. As the **Holy Spirit** leads you to repent and renounce other things, do so earnestly.

Father God, I come to You humbly, acknowledging Your authority and power, and honoring You as creator of heaven and earth. I confess I have operated in idolatry and chose to follow Satan instead of You and Your Word by joining a secret society or attempting to join. I confess and repent of my sin of idolatry and mixing the **holy** with the profane. I repent of taking Your name in vain and the blasphemy attached to being part of a secret society. In the name and power of **Jesus Christ** alone, I repent and renounce all ungodly covenants and association with *Freemasonry*, *Shriners*, the *Illuminati*, lodges, crafts, fraternities, sororities, and any other secret/occult groups pledged by my family and myself.

In the name of **Jesus Christ**, I repent for following and renounce satanism and witchcraft to which I opened myself, and my family to. I renounce the spirits of Baal, Baphomet, Osiris, Isis, Horus, Set, Minerva/Athena, Apollo/Apollyon, Anubis, Bastet, Themis/Atlas, _____ (add in any other names of false gods/goddess attached to the organization). I renounce the spirit of the antichrist, spirits of death, and **ALL** ungodly powers that rule over these organizations.

I repent and renounce rejection, insecurity, and lack of identity in **Christ**, the love of position and power; the love of acceptance, the love of money, the lust of the flesh, the lust of the eyes, and the pride of life that led people into these demonic organizations. I repent and renounce, and break off myself and my family, all fear and intimidation released into participants of these organizations. I recognize the occult ties and ungodliness of these organizations. Through the power of **Jesus Christ**, I repent, renounce, and break all soul ties attached to the people that came from joining these organizations. I pray for all false relationships and friendships You didn't ordain for my life, to cease. I renounce the fear of being alone, the fear of men, and the fear of trusting **God**, in the name of **Jesus Christ**.

I repent and renounce all anxiety, depression, oppression, obsession, emotional damage, confusion, fear of the dark, fear of the light, and fear of sudden noises, etc. I renounce the blinding of spiritual truth, the darkening of the soul, and false imaginations, in **Jesus'** name. I renounce the attack and fear of choking in the night, nightmare spirits, incubus and succubus spirits, every spirit causing asthma, hay fever, emphysema, and breathing difficulty. I repent and renounce emotional hardness, apathy, indifference, unbelief, bitterness, and anger in **Jesus'** name.

I renounce and break the power of the wedding ceremony that married me to the organization (whether literal or spiritual). I repent and renounce every ritual, prayer, and hymn I said, sung, and agreed to, which created a demonic covenant. I repent and renounce the false light mentioned in rituals, which represents Lucifer/Satan. I repent and renounce the worship of the organization instilled in me through initiation. I renounce the spirit of a python trying to squeeze the spiritual life out of me and prevent me from following **The True and Living God** only. I renounce all ancient pagan teachings from Babylon and Egypt and the symbolism attached to secret societies. I renounce the mixing and mingling of truth and error. I acknowledge the mythology, fabrication, and lies taught as truth through these organizations as deception from Satan. I repent and renounce every position held in these organizations by me or anyone in my family. I repent and renounce for calling or thinking of another as a "*master*," or any other similar title that's idolatrous to **God**.

I repent and renounce for taking **Your word** in vain. I repent and renounce vain traditions of men that make the **word of God** of no affect, by accepting initiation and rituals as truth. I repent and renounce for accepting and reciting twisted versions of **God's holy word** made to fit the organization. I repent for swearing an oath to the organization and laying my hand on the **Holy Bible** while pledging myself to the organization. I repent and renounce the curse of all hand signs, calls, secret passwords, handshakes, etc., attached to the organization.

I repent and renounce **ALL** forms of false and ancient religions, polytheism, ancestral worship, philosophy, astrology, astronomy, divination, New Age, Buddhism, Islam, Hinduism, and all demonic powers these secret organizations draw power and strength from. I confess there's only **ONE God**...The **God** of Abraham, Isaac, and

Jacob. Elohim. **The Great I Am**, Who **ALONE** is worthy of all worship and praise. Only through **Jesus Christ, Son of The Living God, The Passover Lamb**, can there be remission of sins, freedom, and redemption. Therefore, I start anew today by giving my life and every part of myself back to You **Jesus**. I thank **You Lord**, all vows, obligations, oaths, penalties, and curses enacted or pronounced against my life and body are removed, ended, and healed in the mighty name of **Jesus**. I thank You, **Father God**, for Your love, mercy, grace, and protection.

In the name of **Jesus Christ**, I pray all these things... **Amen!**

PRAYER FOR DELIVERANCE FROM DECEPTION
(*Isaiah 5:20*)

Lord, I humble myself before you. Reveal to me anything in my life that you're not pleased with. If there is anything in my life that I believe is true but is a lie or anything in my life that I believe is a lie but is true or anything in my life that I believe was evil but was good or anything in my life that I believe was good but was evil, Lord reveal it to me so I can be pleasing to you and not be deceived.

In Jesus Christ's name, Amen!

STRATEGIES TO GET OUT OF SECRET SOCIETIES

Getting individuals out of secret societies is a delicate and often challenging process that requires spiritual discernment, patience, and strategic approaches. Below are expanded strategies to help someone leave these organizations effectively.

1. Fast & Pray For Them

•**Importance of Spiritual Warfare**: Fasting and praying are powerful tools in spiritual warfare. They help to break strongholds and open the person's heart to the truth. (*Matthew 17:21*)

•**Specific Prayers**: Pray specifically for revelation, wisdom, and protection against spiritual deception. Use scripture to guide your prayers, such as *Ephesians 6:12*, which reminds us that our battle is not against flesh and blood.

2. Ask More Questions, Make Fewer Statements About Their Involvement

•**Understanding Their Perspective**: Asking questions helps you understand their perspective and shows you're genuinely interested in their experiences and feelings.

•**Encouraging Self-Reflection**: Questions encourage them to think critically about their involvement and the true nature of the organization. This can lead to self-discovery and openness to leaving.

3. Allow Space & Time For The Holy Spirit To Deal With Them

Patience Is Key: Understand the **Holy Spirit** works in His own time and way. Be patient and trust that **God** is at work in their hearts. (*John 16:8-13*)

Respecting Their Process: Respect their journey and give them the space to process their thoughts and feelings. Avoid pressuring them, which can lead to resistance.

4. Find Other Believers Who Will Commit Themselves To Walk With You Through This Process

Building A Support Network: Having a support network of believers can provide encouragement, prayer, and practical help. (*Galatians 6:2*)

Accountability: A community offers accountability and ensures you're not carrying the burden alone. It also provides additional perspectives and insights.

5. Be Led By The Holy Spirit When & How To Approach Them

Discernment: Pray for discernment on the right moments to speak and the right words to say. The **Holy Spirit** will guide you to be sensitive to their needs and timing. (*Luke 12:12*)

Spirit-Led Conversations: Trust the **Holy Spirit** will lead your conversations and give you the wisdom to address your concerns effectively.

6. Watch Out For The Spirit of Offense

Guarding Your Heart: Stay vigilant against the spirit of offense, which can distract and discourage you. Remember their reactions are often a defense mechanism. (*Proverbs 4:23*)

Responding With Grace: Respond to their words and actions with grace and love, keeping in mind that you're battling spiritual forces, not the individual. (*Ephesians 4:31-32*)

7. Educate Them On The Truth of Scripture

Biblical Teachings: Provide them with scriptural truths that counter the teachings and practices of the secret society. Use verses that highlight God's view on idolatry, oaths, and allegiance.

Study Together: Offer to study the **Bible** together, focusing on passages that reveal God's truth and love. This can open their eyes to the inconsistencies between their faith and the secret society's teachings.

8. Expose The Deceptions of The Secret Society

Reveal Hidden Truths: Share factual information and testimonies from ex-members that expose the deceptive practices and beliefs of the secret society.

Highlight Contradictions: Point out contradictions between the society's teachings and the **Bible**, helping them see the falsehoods they have been taught.

9. Provide Resources For Healing & Deliverance

Counseling and Support: Recommend **Christian** counseling or support groups that specialize in helping people leave *Deliverance Ministry* cults and secret societies. If appropriate, connect them with a deliverance ministry that can help them break free from spiritual bondage.

10. Encourage Repentance & Renunciation

Renouncing Oaths: Guide them through the process of renouncing oaths or covenants they made with the secret society. Emphasize the importance of verbally breaking these agreements in **Jesus'** name.

Repentance: Encourage them to repent for their involvement and seek God's forgiveness and cleansing. (*1 John 1:9*)

11. Celebrate Small Victories

Acknowledge Progress: Recognize and celebrate any steps they take towards leaving the society, no matter how small. This can provide encouragement and motivation.

Continued Support: Continue to support and pray for them after they leave the secret society, as the journey to full freedom and healing may take time.

By implementing these strategies, you can effectively support individuals in breaking free from the bondage of secret societies and guide them toward a life of freedom in **Christ**.

Twelve (12) Evil Spirits That Oppose Truth

Jesus declared Himself to be "*the way, the truth, and the life*" (*John 14:6*). Throughout His ministry, He faced various evil spirits that sought to undermine, distort, and oppose the truth He embodied and proclaimed. These same spirits continue to oppose anyone who speaks the truth and those who are presented with it. Recognizing these spirits and their tactics helps believers stand firm in the truth and resist deception.

1. The Spirit of Deception

John 8:44 "You belong to your father, the devil, and you want to carry out your father's desires. He was a murderer from the beginning, not holding to the truth, for there is no truth in him. When he lies, he speaks his native language, for he is a liar and the father of lies."

The spirit of deception blinds people to the truth making it difficult to distinguish between good and evil. It twists reality, creating confusion and leading people away from the path of righteousness. This spirit opposes those who speak the truth by spreading lies and misinformation, causing others to doubt and reject the truth.

2. The Spirit of Pride

Matthew 23:5-12 "Everything they do is done for people to see: They make their phylacteries wide and the tassels on their garments long; they love the place of honor at banquets and the most important seats in the synagogues; they love to be greeted with respect in the marketplaces and to be called 'Rabbi' by others."

The spirit of pride is characterized by an unwillingness to admit wrong or to let go of one's ego. It seeks recognition and validation from others rather than from **God**. This spirit opposes the truth by fostering arrogance and self-righteousness, preventing individuals from humbling themselves to accept and follow the truth.

3. The Spirit of Accusation

John 8:6 "They were using this question as a trap, in order to have a basis for accusing him. But Jesus bent down and started to write on the ground with his finger."

The spirit of accusation deflects attention from oneself by pointing fingers at others. It seeks to entrap and condemn, as seen in the Pharisees' attempts to accuse **Jesus** of wrongdoing. This spirit opposes the truth by focusing on fault-finding and condemnation, creating an environment of mistrust and hostility.

4. The Spirit of Offense

Matthew 13:57 "And they took offense at him. But Jesus said to them, 'A prophet is not without honor except in his own town and in his own home.'"

The spirit of offense causes individuals to become angry or resentful due to perceived insults or slights. It leads to rejection and hostility towards the message and messenger of **God**. This spirit opposes the truth by stirring up feelings of hurt and resentment, causing people to reject the truth and those who present it.

5. The Spirit of Fear

John 19:38 "Later, Joseph of Arimathea asked Pilate for the body of Jesus. Now Joseph was a disciple of Jesus, but secretly because he feared the Jewish leaders."

The spirit of fear paralyzes individuals, making them indecisive and reluctant to act. It prevents people from standing up for their beliefs and following God's will. This spirit opposes the truth by instilling fear and doubt, discouraging people from embracing and proclaiming the truth boldly.

6. The Spirit of Murder

John 8:40 "As it is, you are looking for a way to kill me, a man who has told you the truth that I heard from God. Abraham did not do such things."

The spirit of murder seeks to destroy and eliminate those who stand for truth and righteousness. It fosters hatred and violence, as seen in the religious leaders' plots to kill **Jesus**. This spirit opposes the truth by seeking to silence and remove those who boldly proclaim it.

7. The Spirit of Unbelief

Mark 6:6 "He was amazed at their lack of faith. Then Jesus went around teaching from village to village."

The spirit of unbelief is marked by doubt and a lack of faith. It rejects the evidence of God's power and presence, leading to spiritual stagnation. This spirit opposes the truth by fostering skepticism and disbelief, preventing people from accepting and acting upon the truth.

8. The Spirit of Jealousy

*Mark 15:10 "**Knowing it was out of self-interest that the chief priests had handed Jesus over to him**."*

The spirit of jealousy breeds envy and resentment towards others' success or favor. It drives individuals to undermine and oppose those they perceive as threats. This spirit opposes the truth by creating division and competition, preventing people from working together to advance the truth.

9. The Spirit of Rejection

*John 1:11 "**He came to that which was his own, but his own did not receive him**."*

The spirit of rejection causes individuals to spurn and marginalize others, making them feel unworthy and unwanted. It leads to feelings of isolation and worthlessness. This spirit opposes the truth by causing people to reject the message and messengers of **God**, leading to spiritual alienation.

10. The Spirit of Intimidation

John 9:22 "His parents said this because they were afraid of the Jewish leaders, who already had decided that anyone who acknowledged that Jesus was the Messiah would be put out of the synagogue."

The spirit of intimidation seeks to control and silence through fear and coercion. It prevents people from expressing their faith and standing up for the truth. This spirit opposes the truth by instilling fear of repercussions, discouraging people from speaking and living out the truth.

11. The Spirit of Belittling

John 7:52 "They replied, 'Are you from Galilee, too? Look into it, and you will find that a prophet does not come out of Galilee.'"

The spirit of belittling degrades and dismisses others, often based on their background or perceived inferiority. It undermines and discredits, as seen in the Pharisees' dismissal of Jesus because of His Galilean origin. This spirit opposes the truth by diminishing the worth and contributions of others.

12. The Spirit of Blasphemy

Matthew 12:24 "But when the Pharisees heard this, they said, 'It is only by Beelzebul, the prince of demons, that this fellow drives out demons.'"

The spirit of blasphemy is characterized by irreverence and mockery of the divine. It attributes the works of **God** to evil sources, as demonstrated by the Pharisees' accusation that **Jesus** cast out demons by the power of Beelzebul. This spirit opposes the truth by discrediting and dishonoring the holy.

Conclusion

These evil spirits that opposed Jesus continue to oppose the truth today. By recognizing their tactics, believers can stand firm in the truth and resist the influences that seek to lead them astray. Understanding these opposing forces equips us to uphold the truth of the Gospel, combat spiritual deception, and live lives that glorify God.

SUPPORT GROUPS

EX BLGO Union

https://www.facebook.com/groups/2211768471/

Out From Among Them Ministries Support Group

https://www.facebook.com/groups/1084098125092778/

https://www.outfromamongthem.com/

RECOMMENDED BOOKS

Blessing or Curse: You Can Choose by Derek Prince

Evil Altars - Deliverance from the Spirit of Fraternity by Pastor A.W. "Al" Barlow, Esquire

The Answer: God's Call To Leave Secret Societies

Made in the USA
Columbia, SC
23 January 2025